T0207782

More
and
More

"Climbing the Mountain to Infinity"

Walter Alan Ray

MORE AND MORE
"CLIMBING THE MOUNTAIN TO INFINITY"

Scripture quotations are from The Holy Bible, English Standard Version®, copyright © 2001 by Crossway Bibles, a publishing ministry of Good News Publishers. Used by permission. All rights reserved.

iUniverse books may be ordered through booksellers or by contacting:

iUniverse
1663 Liberty Drive
Bloomington, IN 47403
www.iuniverse.com
844-349-9409

ISBN: 978-1-6632-3608-1 (sc)
ISBN: 978-1-6632-3609-8 (e)

Library of Congress Control Number: 2022903176

Print information available on the last page.

iUniverse rev. date: 03/04/2022

Filled with a plethora of biblical wisdom and practical application, Walter Ray's new book *More and More* is great book about practical Christian living. It's my pleasure to recommend it to anyone serious about growing closer to Christ.

—Tim Peck
Senior Pastor, Glenkirk Church

Walter Ray takes you on a journey which begins by asking if you have ever had that sneaking suspicion that there is more to your faith than you are currently experiencing? With significant insight and wisdom Dr. Ray then enables you to examine passages of scripture which wrestle with the value of free will, the sovereignty of God, the debilitating nature of racism, the heart of the Gospel, how to respond when disaster strikes, the existence of evil, and actively discerning God's will. If you are looking for a good read that will cause you to think and think deeply about your life and the centrality of faith in it, this may well be a book for you.

—Dr. Richard Gibbons
Senior Pastor, First Presbyterian Church
Greenville, South Carolina

With great joy and admiration, I dedicate
this book to my wife Paula.

An excellent wife who can find?
She is far more precious than jewels.
The heart of her husband trusts in her,
and he will have no lack of gain.
She does him good, and not harm,
all the days of her life.

Proverbs 33:10-12

CONTENTS

INTRODUCTION

Why Read This Book?

"I will make with them an everlasting covenant,
that I will not turn away from doing good to them."

Jeremiah 32:40

I was walking across a narrow ledge about six inches wide. The ledge went on for about ten feet along the nearly vertical side of a mountain. I was leading my wife. We held hands. If we fell, it would be about a two hundred foot fall onto jagged rocks. My heart was in my mouth, and I was silently screaming, Help us, O God!

How did we get into such a position? Why in the world were we doing such a crazy thing? I will explain later how we arrived in this predicament. The reason I bring it up now is because it can convey to you what I believe is *the most important benefit you can derive from reading this book.*

As we go through life we will face many obstacles and difficult times. How is it possible to face these trials with enough faith to believe that God is always working good on our behalf. Can my faith be strong enough to believe this? *The prime objective of this book is to show you how to grow in your faith so that no matter what trial you are enduring, you might have faith enough to believe that God is with you, and at that very moment God is working good on your behalf. So you may praise him more and more.*

This book has been a sixty-three year journey. I started my journey with Jesus Christ at the age of twenty-one while I was a graduate student in electrical engineering at MIT. Up until that time, I considered myself to be an agnostic. Some years after I began my journey with Jesus Christ, I came across a quotation by E. Stanley Jones: "I am 83, and I'm more excited today about being a Christian than I was at 18 when I put my feet upon the Way."[1] At the time I read this, I thought, *How powerful! Could this become true for me?*

As I write this book today, I can say about myself, "I am eighty-five, and I am more excited today about being a Christian than I was at twenty-one when I put my feet upon the *way.*"

As I look back at my sixty-four years of journey since being introduced to Jesus Christ, I can say it has been a journey of progressively learning more about the wonders of God. *More and more* is the goal of someone who has made contact with the infinite God and who now seeks to progress to a deeper more mature level. The deepest level of experience with God is something that we will not fully achieve in this lifetime, but along with Paul the Apostle, we can approach it. As far as Paul had advanced in the Christian life at the time he wrote Philippians, he knew that there was considerably more progress ahead.

Growing more and more in Christ is a journey of sanctification; It is the journey of being transformed into the likeness of Jesus

---

[1] E. Stanley Jones, *A Song of Ascents*, (Tennessee, Abingdon Press, 1968), 20.

Christ. It is a wild journey. It is more difficult and challenging than climbing the highest point of the Matterhorn (Yes, I did!). It is not a straight-line ascent. It involves dizzying heights and severe trials, rights and lefts, and easts and wests. But once we have started this journey, we yearn for more.

> O God, you are my God; earnestly I seek you; my soul thirsts for you; my flesh faints for you.
>
> Psalm 63:1

Let us begin this journey. It is a journey on which it is not possible to exhaust any part of it. You cannot become bored on this journey because you will be making contact with the infinite God. The reality and power of his presence is always more than we think it can be. It is my prayer that as you read this book, you will, with the aid of the Holy Spirit, make significant progress on this journey.

Infinite progression.
More and more.

CHAPTER 1
Paul Says There is "Much More"

And better thence again, and better still, in infinite
progression...

John Milton[2]

M any people think that when they believe in Christ as Lord
and Savior, they have arrived. And yet a great surprise is
coming. There is more ahead. More and more. The words of John
Milton, "and better still, in infinite progression," deal with the
nature of our infinite God. When he crafted the words "and better
still, in infinite progression," perhaps Milton was influenced by the
phrase *more and more* in Psalm 71:14, which says, "But I will hope
continually and will praise you yet more and more."

---

[2] John Milton, *The Beauties of Milton,* (Thompson and Young, Printed for the
Company of Booksellers, 1783), Volume I, p. 205

How amazing that there is not a limit in the words "more and more." How startling that we cannot say, "I have reached the end. There I see it, I just passed it!" In a race, we say, "I have crossed the finish line." But when I deal with Jesus Christ, there is no summit; there is only more and more. There is only infinite progression. What strange goal is this that cannot be reached? What a strange finish line it is that it cannot be crossed. For when I do cross it, behold, there is more. And not only more, but *more and more*. What a treasure of hidden joy! More and more. The taste grows more savory in front of my very eyes. He is reaching out to us. His love seeks to reach us more and more. Yes, Lord, your love for me is more and more. Reach me. Touch me. Now.

The closer I get to Jesus Christ, the more intimately I want to know him. The more I praise him, the more fully I realize how great he is. The better I know him, the more I want to experience his love and character and personality. This is the infinite progression. The further along I progress, the more there remains to advance! "And better thence again, and better still, in infinite progression" (quotation by John Milton in this chapter). And when all is said and done, I have not yet reached the final point of my journey because there is *more and more*.

There is more to the Christian life than what you have experienced at this point in your life. This book hopes to give you some guidance on how to progress up this mountain toward the infinite God. Climbing the mountain toward infinity.

Not only is there more, but there is *more and more*.

In the councils of heaven, before time began, God addressed the question, How shall I show them my love? The answer God gave was this: "I will give myself to die for them."

God shows his love for us in that while we were still sinners, Christ died for us.

Romans 5:8

Paul refers to this great act of love in Romans 5:8, and then there is yet another colossal surprise, for he unleashes a divine supernova. Paul tells us that as great as is "the greatest act of love," there is *more*. What? How can it be that there is *more*?

> For if while we were enemies we were reconciled to
> God by the death of his Son, much more, now that
> we are reconciled, shall we be saved by his life.
>
> Romans 5:10

It is an amazing, staggering fact that God has poured out his love upon us by giving his only Son on the cross. That is enough to purchase for us an eternity with God in heaven. Often, those who come to faith in Christ believe they have reached the summit. They believe they have reached the highest point that any faith can reach—eternal life, past sins all forgiven, and contact with a loving God. This is it! I now have heaven on earth!

But that is not all.

There is *more*. There is yet a supernova to come that will surpass in brilliance the light of our being reconciled to God by Christ's death on the cross. I almost hesitate to say it, but this is what Paul said when he uttered the words: "Much more, now that we are reconciled, shall we be saved by his life (Romans 5:10)."

How can it be that the presence of the Lord in our own life gets better and better so that we can praise him more and more? As mature a believer as Paul the Apostle was, he did not believe that he had arrived at any particular level of faith beyond which he could not grow. Paul believed that there was still ample room for growth in his own life as a Christian.

> Not that I have already obtained this or am already
> perfect, but I press on to make it my own. Brothers,
> I do not consider that I have made it my own. But
> one thing I do: forgetting what lies behind and

straining forward to what lies ahead, I press on
toward the goal for the prize of the upward call
of God in Christ Jesus. Let those of us who are
mature think this way, and if in anything you think
otherwise, God will reveal that also to you.

Philippians 3:12–14

Paul wanted more; he wanted to grow in his faith. Paul wanted
to *press on!* Are you satisfied with the degree of Christian growth you
are experiencing in your life? Paul was passionate about his faith, and
he was passionate about his own desire to grow in his journey ("Not
that I have already obtained").

May the Holy Spirit give us a seed of discontent over our rate
of progress in the Christian life. Such a seed of discontent is a good
thing, and we may give him praise for this type of discontent.

A Surprise after Reconciliation

Paul talks about this new journey in Romans 5.

Therefore, since we have been justified by faith,
we have peace with God through our Lord Jesus
Christ. Through him we have also obtained access
by faith into this grace in which we stand, and we
rejoice in hope of the glory of God.

Romans 5:1–2:

Once we are justified by faith and have found peace with
God, another journey begins. We know this from the word *hope* in
Romans 5:2 "We rejoice in hope of the glory of God." The surprising
journey that begins after reconciliation is what we experience as we
"rejoice in hope of the glory of God." Hope is not something that we
already have ("Now hope that is seen is not hope. For who hopes for

what he sees" Romans 8:24), but it is something in the future that we are anticipating. Paul is saying that after we are justified by faith, we rejoice in our hope of the glory of God. We rejoice with great hope as we move into the surprising new journey of experiencing the "glory of God." *Imagine that as you read this book, there will come upon you a power of the Holy Spirit which will transform you into a greater reflection of the glory of God.*

> Beloved, we are God's children now, and what we will be has not yet appeared; but we know that when he appears we shall be like him, because we shall see him as he is.
>
> 1 John 3:2

We are God's children now, but there still remains a further work, for "what we will be has not yet appeared." This additional work results in us being like him when we see him as he is.

There is a continuing work in the believer after coming to Christ for the forgiveness of our sins. I believe the apostle Paul would agree with the statement that there is more to the Christian life than what you and I are experiencing at this moment. I believe Paul knows this because he has experienced it himself in his own life. Paul knew what it meant to say there is yet *much more* for us to experience of God's power in the Christian life. The more I experience of him, the more I want to praise him. The more I praise him, the more I realize how great he is. The better I know him, the more I want to experience his love and character and personality. After Paul had been a Christian for several years, he said,

> Not that I have already obtained this or am already perfect, but I press on to make it my own... But one thing I do: forgetting what lies behind and straining forward to what lies ahead, I press on toward the

goal for the prize of the upward call of God in Christ Jesus.

Philippians 3:12–14

This is the infinite progression. And when all is said and done, I have not yet reached the final point of my journey because there is more. And then, when I reach that, there is more. And more. More and more. And better thence again, and better still, in infinite progression.

If the Death of Christ Saved Us, How Much More Can His Life Do?

The phrase *much more* occurs four times in Romans 5:9–17. Let us look at these four passages from Romans 5 (Romans 5:9, 5:10, 5:15, 5:17). Here is the first one:

> For while we were still weak, at the right time Christ died for the ungodly. For one will scarcely die for a righteous person— though perhaps for a good person one would dare even to die— but God shows his love for us in that while we were still sinners, Christ died for us. Since, therefore, we have now been justified by his blood, *much more* [emphasis added] shall we be saved by him from the wrath of God.
>
> Romans 5:6–9

While we were still sinners, Christ died for us. During the time that we were sinners, before we believed in Christ, Jesus came to redeem us and to die for us. He offered to us the gift of his very life even though we were headed away from him. One would scarcely die for a good person. How much less for a sinful person? And somehow, inexplicably, Christ died for us while we were still sinners on a journey away from God. And after we accepted him, and we became righteous through his blood, *much more* shall we be saved by him. *Much more* will he bring us to the final objective for which he saved us, saving us to the uttermost.

> Consequently, he is able to save to the uttermost those who draw near to God through him, since he always lives to make intercession for them"
>
> Hebrews 7:25

An integral part of saving us to the uttermost is Christ always making intercession for us. What a prayer partner is Jesus! Did you know that he is your personal Prayer Partner, committed to praying daily for you! Let us turn now to the second *much more*.

> For if while we were enemies we were reconciled to God by the death of his Son, *much more* [emphasis added], now that we are reconciled, shall we be saved by his life. More than that, we also rejoice in God through our Lord Jesus Christ, through whom we have now received reconciliation.
>
> Romans 5:10–11

During the very time that we were enemies of God, we were reconciled to God by the death of his Son. The death of Christ was doubly powerful: (a) powerful enough to overcome our being slaves to sin, and (b) powerful enough to turn us around and now lead us toward God. When Christ died and was in the grave, it was his death that brought about our reconciliation. But now it is Christ's life that is at work in us. How *much more*, now that Christ is risen from the dead, shall we be saved by him and brought to that ultimate objective for which he redeemed us! Paul is comparing the effect of the death of Christ with the effect of the life of Christ. If the effect of Christ's *death* was so amazing that it could reconcile us to God, then the effect of Christ's *life* will be multiplied many times! Now to Paul's third use of the words *much more*.

> But the free gift is not like the trespass. For if many died through one man's trespass, *much more* [emphasis added] have the grace of God and the free gift by the grace of that one man Jesus Christ abounded for many. And the free gift is not like the result of that one man's sin. For the judgment following one trespass brought condemnation, but the free gift following many trespasses brought justification.
>
> Romans 5:15–16

Death came through one vehicle, the man Adam. The gift of God's grace came by one vehicle also, the Man Jesus Christ. Comparing the vehicles, we have Adam and Christ. How much more will the result of the one vehicle (Christ) be over the result of the other vehicle (Adam) so that the result brought about by Christ, the gift of free grace, will abound to its recipients? Now the fourth use of *much more*.

> For if, because of one man's trespass, death reigned through that one man, *much more* [emphasis added] will those who receive the abundance of grace and the free gift of righteousness reign in life through the one man Jesus Christ.
>
> Romans 10:17

The trespass of one man initiated the reign of death. The gift of God's abundant grace overcame the reign of death by setting us on the road to our eternal reign. The reign of death came to an end by Christ's death. How *much more*, after Christ died, and because

Christ died, will the reign of humans continue for all eternity? "And they will reign forever and ever" (Revelation 22:5).

Paul's four uses of the words *much more* are similar and related to each other, but if you will look at them carefully, you will see that each one sets forth a different facet of a many-sided jewel.

Romans 5:9 compares what Christ did for us while we were sinners with what Christ will do for us now that we are his. He will do much more than reconciliation accomplished.

Romans 5:10 compares the effect of the death of Christ with the effect Christ can have now that he is risen.

Romans 5:15 compares what is wrought through the man Adam with what is wrought through the risen Christ.

Romans 5:17 compares the reign of death with the reign of Christ.

How much more will the reign of Christ be than the reign of death?

Of the four uses of the words *much more*, each one centered on the death of Christ and the powerful effect of this death. Each time it comes out a little different way, which gives us an added insight and deeper understanding. Paul is "bursting at the seams" to convey the awesome power and great effect of Christ's death on the cross. Paul cannot say it enough times and in enough different ways.

So we find that the four *much more* statements of Romans 5:10–17 lead us into the rarefied atmosphere of beginning to enjoy the results of Christ's death on the cross and the abundant blessings which comprise our reigning forever. Our reign includes:

> And we know that for those who love God all things
> work together for good.
>
> Romans 8:28

> If God is for us, who can be against us?
>
> Romans 8:31

> He who did not spare his own Son but gave him up for us all, how will he not also with him graciously give us all things?
>
> Romans 8:32

> Who shall separate us from the love of Christ? Shall tribulation, or distress, or persecution, or famine, or nakedness, or danger, or sword?
>
> Romans 8:35

> No, in all these things we are more than conquerors through him who loved us. For I am sure that neither death nor life, nor angels nor rulers, nor things present nor things to come, nor powers, nor height nor depth, nor anything else in all creation, will be able to separate us from the love of God in Christ Jesus our Lord.
>
> Romans 8:37–39

All of these items listed above are part of the *much more* that Paul uses in Romans 5:10–19. They are part of the *much more* brought about by the death of Christ.

Do not think that you have yet experienced all that God has available for you. There are higher degrees of experiencing God's glory than you and I can imagine. Ask God to work within you something truly magnificent, and watch him greatly exceed your expectation. All of this is contained in the words *much more*! And my prayer is that you will experience this ascending glory of God as you read this book.

> Now to him who is able to do far more abundantly
> than all that we ask or think, according to the power
> at work within us.

Ephesians 3:20

This is the *much more* that Paul mentions in Romans 5:10. When Christ died, Jesus was at his very lowest point. He emptied himself, taking the form of a servant (Philippians 2:7). He allowed himself to be put to death on a cross (Philippians 2:8). But after he rose from the tomb, he was mighty and triumphant.

> For this reason I bow my knees before the Father, from whom every family in heaven and on earth is named, that according to the riches of his glory he may grant you to be strengthened with power through his Spirit in your inner being, so that Christ may dwell in your hearts through faith— that you, being rooted and grounded in love, may have strength to comprehend with all the saints what is the breadth and length and height and depth, and to know the love of Christ that surpasses knowledge, that you may be filled with all the fullness of God. Now to him who is able to do far more abundantly than all that we ask or think, according to the power at work within us.

Ephesians 3:14–20

Paul prays that the new Christians at Ephesus would experience the *much more* and receive from "the riches of his glory" and that they might be strengthened through the Spirit and comprehend the "breadth and length and height and depth," and to know the love of Christ which surpasses knowledge, and be filled with all the fullness of God. This is truly a sublime prayer, and yet Paul says that all this will pale in splendor compared to the fullness of what God is able to do. Paul believes that God will do far more abundantly than what he has just prayed for the new Christians at Ephesus (see Ephesians 3:20).

At some point in our spiritual journey, we think, "Surely, this must be the ultimate destination." And just when we think we have arrived at the peak of Mount Everest, Paul says, Wait! There is more.

More and more.
Infinite progression.

May you believe, with the Holy Spirit's aid, that as you read this book, he will do far more abundantly than all that you ask or think, according to the power at work within you.

Come, a world of wonder awaits!

For nothing shall be impossible with God. (Jeremiah 32:17)

CHAPTER 2
The Quintessential Heart of The Gospel

> For I delivered to you as of first importance what
> I also received: that Christ died for our sins in
> accordance with the Scriptures,...
>
> 1 Corinthians 15:3

Is there a single most important teaching in the Bible? Many different answers to this question have been proposed by scholars and theologians. Here is the answer given by the Apostle Paul. Paul said that the most important teaching in the Bible is: "Christ died for our sins in accordance with the Scriptures."

> For I delivered to you as of first importance what
> I also received: that Christ died for our sins in
> accordance with the Scriptures,
>
> 1 Corinthians 15:3

It is significant that this teaching appears in the Old Testament, as well as in the New Testament. When Paul says "in accordance with the Scriptures," the word Scriptures is referring to the Old Testament (as the New Testament had not yet been put together).

Every chapter in this book is built upon this central theme that Christ died for our sins. If this teaching is removed, then none of the chapters in this book can stand, or make any sense. If we remove this single teaching from the Bible, then there is no gospel.

The Most Painful Words Ever Uttered

At the moment Christ died on the cross for our sins he uttered words which tell us what he was experiencing at the time. The words are: "My God, my God, why have you forsaken me" (Matthew 27:46). *They are the most painful words ever uttered by anyone in all history.* Never did anyone experience as dolorous a pain as Jesus did when he said "My God, my God, why have you forsaken me?" Never in all of history did anyone speak words more full of anguish than these words of Jesus. What was it that made the cross so painful to Christ? And what was it that made the death of Christ on the cross the most important teaching in the Bible? Let us look first at the question, What made the death on the cross so painful to Christ?

Since the beginning of time, back in eternity, Jesus had enjoyed the glorious presence of the Father. Jesus knew his father's presence well. The Father had said, "This is my beloved Son, with whom I am well pleased (Matthew 3:17)."

I knew that you always hear me,

John 11:42

And he who sent me is with me. He has not left me
alone, for I always do the things that are pleasing
to him."

John 8:29

Jesus had enjoyed this intimate relationship with his father, and
now, suddenly, on the Cross, that glorious presence of the Father was
removed. "Why have you forsaken me?" The presence of the Father
departed from Jesus.

No believer has known the presence of God as Christ knew it.
No saint has enjoyed the love of God as Christ enjoyed it. He had
lived in it, basked in it; there had never been any interruption to it.
Now, as our Lord Jesus Christ had enjoyed the love of God to the
very full, think what it must have been for him to lose that conscious
enjoyment of it. The pain of separation from the Father was strong.

All the tortures of his body he endured in silence; but when it
came to being forsaken of God, then his great heart burst out into
"Lama sabachthani?" His one moan is concerning his God. It is not,
"Why has Peter forsaken me? Why has Judas betrayed me?" These
were sharp griefs, but this is the sharpest. This stroke has cut him to
the quick: "My God, my God, why have you forsaken me?"

Why Was Christ Forsaken By God?

This forsaking was very terrible. Who can fully tell what it is to be
forsaken of God? We can only make a guess for we ourselves have felt
only under a temporary and partial desertion. God has never totally
left us, for Jesus expressly said, "I will never leave you, nor forsake
you" (Hebrews 13:5). Yet we have sometimes felt as if he had cast us
off. We have cried, "Oh, that I knew where I might find him!" Thus
we are able to form some little idea of how the Savior felt when his
God had forsaken him.

Why did Christ experience such a painful death? Certainly there was no reason within him that deserved any such pains. The Bible relates Christ's death to our sins. When Paul gives us the most important teaching in the Bible and says it is "Christ died for our sins," he is relating Christ's death to our sins. The Bible makes it clear on several occasions that there is a close relationship between our sins and Christ's death on the Cross. For instance, looking at Isaiah 53 we find:

> Surely he has borne our griefs and carried our sorrows; yet we esteemed him stricken, smitten by God, and afflicted. But he was pierced for our transgressions; he was crushed for our iniquities; upon him was the chastisement that brought us peace, and with his wounds we are healed. All we like sheep have gone astray; we have turned—every one—to his own way; and the LORD has laid on him the iniquity of us all.
>
> Isaiah 53:4-6

Paul describes the relationship between Christ's death on the cross and our sins in the following manner:

> Therefore, we are ambassadors for Christ, God making his appeal through us. We implore you on behalf of Christ, be reconciled to God. For our sake he made him to be sin who knew no sin, so that in him we might become the righteousness of God.
>
> 2 Corinthians 5:20-21

> For while we were still weak, at the right time Christ died for the ungodly...
>
> Romans 5:6

but God shows his love for us in that while we were still sinners, Christ died for us…

Romans 5:8

He who did not spare his own Son but gave him up for us all, how will he not also with him graciously give us all things?

Romans 8:32

the Lord Jesus Christ, who gave himself for our sins to deliver us from the present evil age, according to the will of our God and Father, to whom be the glory forever and ever. Amen.

Galatians 1:4-5

And then in the writings of Peter:

He himself bore our sins in his body on the tree,
That we might die to sin and live to righteousness.
By his wounds you have been healed.

1 Peter 2:24

Peter, Paul, and Isaiah state that there is a relationship between Christ's death on the Cross and our sins. And that relationship is: our sins are forgiven because Christ died on the cross. And there are many other places in the Bible where this same truth is presented (Zechariah 12:10, John 19:37, Revelation 1:7, Matthew 20:28, John 10:11, John 10:15, John 15:13, John 3:16, 1 John 3:16, Romans 4:25, Galatians 2:20, 1 Timothy 2:6, Titus 2:14, 1 Peter 1:18-19). All these Scriptures lead us directly to what Paul said is the most important teaching in the Bible: Christ died for our sins. It is significant to note that *there is no other place in the entire Bible where a particular teaching is said to be the most important teaching in the Bible!* The only place in the Bible where a passage claims to be giving us the most important teaching in the Bible is in 1 Corinthians 15:3. And that teaching is: <u>Christ died for our sins</u>. Our sins can be forgiven because Christ died on the cross. There is no other means given in the Bible whereby our sins can be forgiven.

How Did Christ's Death Bring About The Forgiveness of Our Sins?

The words of Jesus: "my God, my God, why have you forsaken me" show us what it is about Christ's death on the cross that brings about the forgiveness of our sins. It is the pain that Christ suffered on the Cross. It is that which caused him to cry out with that most anguished cry: "My God, why have you forsaken me?"

This was the hour in which Christ was made to stand before God as the sin-bearer, according to that ancient prophecy,

> and the LORD has laid on him the iniquity of us all.
>
> Isaiah 53:6

> and he shall bear their iniquities.
>
> Isaiah 53:11

Peter puts it, "He himself bore our sins in his body on the tree" (1 Peter 2:24). Christ had no sin of his own; but the Lord had "laid on him the iniquity of us all." This was the agonizing pain which Christ experienced when he was dying on the cross.

The meaning of the words "Christ died for our sins" is simple, yet unfathomable. It is simple enough for a child to understand ("unless you come to me as a child...," Mark 10:15), and yet it is deep enough for the greatest intellectual giant to fall short of its full comprehension. *The more fully we comprehend and accept the significance of Christ's death on the Cross, the more closely will we come to the infinite God*, and greater will be our transformation into the likeness of Christ (1 John 3:2).

When Jesus cried out those words he still said "*My* God." There was no diminution of faith on the part of Jesus. He still called the Father, "My God."

"Why hast thou forsaken me?" Did not Jesus know? Did he not know why he was forsaken? Yes. Jesus knew why.

In Matthew 20:28 Jesus said "the Son of Man came not to be served but to serve, and to give his life a ransom for many", and in John 10:15, he said "I lay down my life for the sheep."

He knew why the Father had forsaken him, but in his humanity, the intense pain of separation must have startled and shocked him, so he cried out. At this very moment Jesus "bore the sin of many (Isa 53:12)." At this moment "The Lord has laid on him the iniquity of us all (Isaiah 53:6)." And so, it was the bearing of our sins upon his body that brought to him the great anguish that caused him to say "My God, My God, why have you forsaken me?" God's holiness will not share space with sin ("but your iniquities have made a separation between you and your God" Isaiah 59:2).

What was the reason for it? Our Savior could answer his own question. If for a moment, Christ in his humanity was perplexed, he soon came to a clear understanding, for he said, "It is finished". Why, then, did God forsake his Son? No answer makes any sense other than: *Jesus stood in our stead*. There was no reason in Christ why the Father should forsake him. He was perfect, and his life was without spot. Since there were no reasons in the character and person of the Lord Jesus why his Father should forsake him, we must look elsewhere. The reason the father forsook him was because our sins were laid upon Jesus.

It is impossible to put into human words the full extent of what Christ suffered when he was excluded from the presence of God. Christ was divine. He was one with the Father. To remove Christ from the presence of the Father was to take a large part of Christ away from him. This stripping of Christ from the God-part of his nature must have been painful beyond what any human words can describe. Christ did this willingly because of his great love for us.

God the Father could have given himself to die for our sins, but he did something even more wonderful. He gave his own son to die for us. When a father truly loves and adores his son, it is easier for the father to sustain an injury himself than to see his son injured. *It was more difficult for God the Father to give his Son, than to offer himself as a redemption for us.* This shows the extent of the Father's love for us. He loved us so much that he gave his most valuable possession for us.

As to my sin, I hear its harsh accusing no more when I hear Jesus cry, "Why hast thou forsaken me?" I know that I deserve separation from God at the hand of God's justice, but I am not afraid. He will never forsake me, for he forsook his Son on my behalf. I shall not suffer for my sin, for Jesus has suffered to the full in my stead.

Christ suffered more on the Cross than can possibly be conveyed by human words. The reason Christ suffered on the Cross was to atone for the total weight of all the sins of humanity. This means that Christ suffered the consequences of all the sins of all the people who ever lived. Christ did not suffer the consequence of the sins of one person only, but the sins of *all* the people who ever lived. If Christ's pain on the Cross was greater than you and I can ever understand, this must also mean that the actual extent and weight of our own sin is greater than you and I can ever imagine.

There are many people today who believe that Christ's death on the Cross was merely a supreme moral example for us. They take it as a sacrifice whose purpose was to inspire us to live a sacrificial life that gives to others. But according to Paul the apostle, if we think this is the main point of Christ's death on the Cross, then we have totally missed the point. The point is that Christ's death on the Cross is what allows our sins to be forgiven. This is the doctrine of the atonement.

This point is a stumbling block to many who investigate the teachings of the Bible. C.S. Lewis made the journey from agnostic to believer in Christ. At one point Lewis wrote:

"So even if he rose from the dead, what I couldn't understand was how the life and death of Someone Else (whoever he was) 2000 years ago could help us here and now."[3]

Lewis was wrestling with the concept of the Atonement: that the death of Jesus Christ somehow brought about the forgiveness of our sins if we accept him as our Savior and Lord. Lewis did not see how this was supposed to "work," and until he figured this out, he did not see how he could embrace Christianity. Lewis had a fascinating dinner with Tolkien and Dyson, two good friends of C.S. Lewis, who helped him to embrace the atonement of Christ (JRR Tolkien, wrote "Lord of the Rings" and "The Hobbit", while Hugo Dyson was an English don at the University of Reading).[4]

There are many different theories as to how Christ's death on the Cross could bring about God's forgiveness of our sins. It is interesting to me that neither Lewis nor Jacobs (Alan Jacobs is an expert on CS Lewis, and wrote "The Narnian", on the life of Lewis) offers any explanation of how this can be. It may be that certain different portions of many different theories of atonement combine to form the ultimate and correct theory. I personally do not profess to have an the ultimate theory of how the atonement "works." But I do believe this with all the certainty that my heart and mind can muster: *Christ's death on the Cross is what makes it possible for me to have my sins forgiven by God.*

We have a choice between these two alternatives: 1) Accept Christ's death on the cross as the means of dealing with the consequences of our sins, or 2) *we* will provide for the consequence of our sins by our own means. Before our eyes are opened by the

---

[3] Alan Jacobs, *The Narnian*, (New York, Harper Collins Publisher, 2005), 147. For further discussion of Lewis's Views, see page 148.

[4] Op. cit. See pp. 148-149 for this interesting discussion by Jacobs about Lewis's view of the atonement.

power of the Holy Spirit we think that the consequences of our sins cannot be very significant in the eyes of a loving God and so we do not hesitate to say that we can deal with this in our own strength and wisdom. But there is an enormous problem here in that Jesus, by his words "My God, my God, why have you forsaken me?" has shown us the consequence of our sins. The consequence of our sins is separation from God. This is what Jesus experienced when he took upon himself our sins. He experienced separation from God so strongly that he cried out "My God, My God, why have you forsaken me?" If we insist upon dealing with the consequence of our sins in our own strength, then we will experience separation from God.

It could be argued that the consequence of sin that Jesus experienced was not eternal. It only lasted while he was on the cross, and in the tomb (three days). True, but we need to keep in mind that Jesus, the Son of God, was equal to God the Father (see John 10:27-30). Jesus is a Being who is infinite in all his characteristics. So when Jesus experienced God the Father forsaking him for a short time, that was a consequence infinite in size, although not infinite in duration. Since we are not infinite in size (we are not God), for us to experience a consequence of sin which would be equal to what Jesus experienced, then we would need to experience it forever. This is exactly what the Bible teaches.

To summarize, here is what Christ experienced when he made the statement "My God, My God, why hast thou forsaken me?" He experienced the consequence of our sins. "He himself bore our sins in his body on the tree." The implication is: If he had not borne our sins in his body then we would have had to bear our sins. We would have had to suffer what Christ suffered for us. We would have had to experience the agony which Christ experienced. Many times in the Bible it is taught that the consequence of our sins is laid upon the Messiah.

It is of vital importance that we realize Christ's death on the Cross was unlike any other death on the Cross. Many people have suffered death on the Cross, in fact it was one of various means of putting people to death in the first century. *But no death other than Christ's was able to atone for the sins of another person.* Christ's death on the Cross was infinitely more painful to Christ than any other person's death on a Cross was to that person. The words of Christ "Why have you forsaken me" expressed the greatest pain ever experienced by anyone in the entire history of the world. The reason Christ's death on the Cross was so painful is because on the Cross Christ actually experienced a separation from God, a full and complete separation from God his Father. This separation from God the Father came after Christ had experienced full and total intimacy with God the Father for immeasurable ages – from the beginning.

Please do not soliloquize, *Oh, I am not that bad. I have not committed such great sins as all that. Why, I am not like these other sinners who are extortioners, unjust, adulterers.*

Careful!

You are beginning to sound like the tax collector in Luke 18:13. The truth is that you and I have indeed committed the sins which made it necessary for Christ to die such a painful death on the cross.

Jesus knew that he was going to die on the cross for our sins. In the Garden of Gethsemane Jesus began to feel the awful shadow of his impending death, for he said "My Father, if it be possible, let this cup pass from me." (Matt 26:39). Jesus knew it was going to be exceedingly painful. But Jesus had not yet experienced this pain on the Cross, so he did not know precisely how painful it would be. As a result of his omniscience Jesus knew in his mind that the death on the Cross would be exceedingly painful, but he had not yet experienced in his body the pain of that death.

When the pain actually came on the Cross, Jesus was so startled by its intensity that he cried out, "God, why have you forsaken me?" The pain of bearing our sins was even worse than he expected. *There is no way that Christ could have experienced a greater pain on the Cross than the actual pain which he experienced.* He experienced the greatest pain that it was possible for him to experience. This pain was brought about by the fact that God (the Father) totally abandoned him. Hence his words "Why have you forsaken me?" God had totally withdrawn his presence from Christ. This is the cost of Christ paying the price for our sins. The cost for dealing with these sins was so great, that the weight of the sins themselves must have been enormous!

It is impossible for us to have even the slightest idea of the extent of our sins without the supernatural enlightening power of the Holy Spirit. The convicting (enlightening) power of the Holy Spirit is the only power that can make us aware of the extent of our sin.

> Nevertheless, I tell you the truth: it is to your advantage that I go away, for if I do not go away, the Helper will not come to you. But if I go, I will send him to you. And when he comes, he will convict the world concerning sin and righteousness and judgment: concerning sin, because they do not believe in me; concerning righteousness, because I go to the Father, and you will see me no longer; concerning judgment, because the ruler of this world is judged.
>
> John 16:7-11

Why We Need An Awareness Of The Greatness Of Our Sins

In order to grow in our understanding of Christ's death on the Cross, we must grow in our appreciation of the enormity of our sins. And this can only happen by the enlightenment of the Holy Spirit. So we need to pray, "Holy Spirit, please help me to see more clearly the darkness of my past sins, and the depth of the pain which my sins have brought to Jesus Christ."

There is a reason why it is so important for us to be aware of how much our Lord suffered on the cross. This has a direct proportionate effect on the degree of our thanksgiving to Christ and of our love for Christ. Jesus explained this in Luke 7. Jesus tells a story in Luke 7:40-50 about a money lender who lends money to two people. To one he loans five hundred denarii and to the other he loans fifty denarii. Neither one can repay the debt. He forgives them both. Jesus then asks Peter, which do you think was more grateful? Simon answers, the one for whom he cancelled the larger debt. Jesus said, "you have answered correctly." Then Jesus referred to the woman he had just forgiven and said, "Your sins which are many, are forgiven." Jesus is teaching that if the sins forgiven are many, the person will love much, and that he who is forgiven little, loves little."

We can conclude from this that the more aware we are of the depth of the sins we have committed the more we will love Jesus Christ, the forgiver. So we can see the importance of being aware of the enormity of our sins before God. If we think our sins are little, then we love him "a little" for his forgiveness.

We find a parallel situation in Ezekiel chapter 16:2, where the Lord says to Ezekiel: "Son of man, make known to Jerusalem her abominations." Jerusalem had turned away from the Lord, and was engaged in sins of an egregious nature. Jerusalem was living in abject ignorance about her sins. The first step in God's healing work was for Jerusalem to become aware of and acknowledge the seriousness of her sin. So the Lord assigned to Ezekiel the difficult task of making clear to Jerusalem the nature of her sin. We are shocked by what Ezekiel says. We can hardly believe it. The debasement attributed to Jerusalem is of a most embarrassing nature. It would be highly embarrassing for a minister to feel called to preach a sermon on the abominations of Jerusalem that are mentioned in Ezekiel 16. And yet Ezekiel spells it out.

> How sick is your heart, declares the Lord God, because you did all these things, the deeds of a brazen prostitute, building your vaulted chamber at the head of every street, and making your lofty place in every square. Yet you were not like a prostitute,

because you scorned payment. Adulterous wife, who receives strangers instead of her husband! Men give gifts to all prostitutes, but you gave your gifts to all your lovers, bribing them to come to you from every side with your whorings. So you were different from other women in your whorings. No one solicited you to play the whore, and you gave payment, while no payment was given to you; therefore you were different.

Ezekiel 16:30-34

They gave their sons and daughters for burned sacrifices (Ezekiel 16:20-12). They built vaulted chambers (Ezekiel 16:23) on the street corner, and there offered themselves to any passerby (Ezekiel 16:25) and multiplied their whoring. Jerusalem was an adulterous wife, who received strangers instead of her husband, and she was even worse than a prostitute who received money from others for she did not receive payment, but instead gave payment to men for her whorings with them. By directly and openly charging Jerusalem with their sins, Ezekiel hoped to bring them to a realization of how brazenly they were violating God's commands, with the hoped for result being the repentance of their sins. Jesus said the sins of Jerusalem were worse than the sins of Sodom and Gomorrah.

Truly, I say to you, it will be more bearable on the day of judgment for the land of Sodom and Gomorrah than for that town.

Matthew 10:15

Their sins were so outrageous that they made Sodom and Gomorrah seem more righteous than they! Jerusalem's sins were so vile that in comparison, the sins of both Sodom and Samaria seemed almost like righteous deeds. (See Ezekiel 16:49-52).

No doubt when many churchgoers read of the sins in Ezekiel 16 they are dismayed and shocked, thinking, *I am glad that I am not guilty of such transgressions. Ezekiel is surely talking about others, not people like myself.*

I think most of us would agree that the sins of Jerusalem listed in Ezekiel 16, on a scale of 1-10 (with a "ten" being the absolute worst sin we could commit) would rank very near to 10. And we comfortingly say to ourselves, I am glad that I am nowhere near a ten, but maybe rank about a five or six.

This is not to make you feel that you have sinned as egregiously as hiring a prostitute, or to make you feel that if you have never been with a prostitute, you might as well, because you have already committed a sin equal to that. The Apostle Paul acknowledges that there is some logic behind this proposition, but he rejects it at once!

> Now the law came in to increase the trespass, but where sin increased, grace abounded all the more, so that, as sin reigned in death, grace also might reign through righteousness leading to eternal life through Jesus Christ our Lord. What shall we say then? Are we to continue in sin that grace may abound? By no means! How can we who died to sin still live in it?
>
> Romans 5:20-6:2

The greatest sin we can commit is to break the greatest commandment. Jesus said the greatest commandment is to love God with all your heart. If we do not love God with all our heart, then we are loving other gods more than the one and only true God. This is often referred to in the Old Testament as going after other gods, or whoring after other gods.

> My people inquire of a piece of wood, and their walking staff gives them oracles. For a spirit of

27

> whoredom has led them astray, and they have left
> their God to play the whore.
>
> Hosea 4:12

See also, Exodus 34:16, Ezekiel 20:30, Nahum 3:4,
Deuteronomy 31:16.

Here follows another observation on how we can appreciate
more fully the depth of our sin.

> ...but we know that when he appears we shall be like
> him, because we shall see him as he is.
>
> 1 John 3:2

From 1 John 3:2 we see that when he comes again, we shall see
him face to face and we shall become like him. In our humanity,
before we are fully transformed into the image of Jesus Christ (when
we see him face to face), we are still an *infinite* distance from being
like Jesus Christ (since he is infinite in his power, his goodness, his
holiness, his purity, and in every characteristic which is listed in
Galatians 5:22 as a "fruit of the Spirit.") This explains a strange
phenomenon which well-known saints of history agree upon: that
the more we grow as Christians, the more we realize our sinfulness
and the extent of our sin. One might think that as we grow in our
spiritual journey and become more holy, the extent to which we
feel our sin would be diminished. In one sense we do become more
holy, but that is only when our standard of comparison is our self.
When our standard of comparison is Jesus Christ then the more we
are transformed into his likeness, the more we realize how great a
distance still separates us from being Christ-like.

As we journey closer to our end, we grow spiritually (this
includes growth in the degree of our spiritual perception). That
means that the closer we get to the end of our lives, because our
spiritual perception is now more mature, the more clearly we can

perceive that there is still an infinite distance remaining between us and Jesus Christ, and so we are then *more* aware of our sin! This leaves us with the seemingly paradoxical situation that the more we grow in our actual spirituality, the more aware we become of the depth of our sin. This makes clear the importance of understanding that my own sins were weighty enough to send Jesus Christ to his death on the cross. And the deeper is my understanding of this truth, the greater is my love for my forgiver.

I need to pray that the Holy Spirit will open my eyes to the extent of my own personal sin. And so I ask the Holy Spirit to help me realize that I am deserving of being separated from God for all eternity, but not that I be driven mad by a sense of my sin. For let us never forget that in Christ we are now *white as snow*. Our value is so great that Christ gave himself on our behalf, and the Lord said: "you are precious in my sight," Isaiah 43:3.

Keep in mind that in Christ we are forgiven for all our sins. We are not forgiven depending upon how fully we understand the depth of our sin. We are forgiven because Christ died for all of our sins, and we accept God's forgiveness for our sins, although we do not have a full awareness and appreciation of the terrible weight of our sins. God has laid on him the iniquity of us all. How fully we understand the enormity of the weight of our sin does have an effect upon how fully we experience the "riches of Christ" (Ephesians). By faith in Christ we are forgiven, not by the extent of our understanding of the weight of our sin, but because Christ died for our sins. Our understanding of the Cross does have an effect on the amount of praise we can give to him, and hence upon the degree to which we experience *the riches of Christ*!!!

So let us pray: Holy Spirit help me become more aware of the heavy weight of my sin, in order that I may have a greater appreciation of the great weight that Christ bore on the Cross, and that I may praise you more and more for the gift of salvation.

Many believers, especially in the early part of their journey with Christ, believe that their sins are relatively minor and not of much importance. If this is the case, then they will think that God's love for them is also relatively minor, because Christ's grief on the Cross need only have been rather *light* in order to atone for our *light sins*. But the greater I realize the depth of my sins, then the greater also do I realize what Christ's suffering must have been to atone for these sins. The greater his suffering, then the greater his grief on the Cross. The greater his grief on the Cross, the greater will be my thanksgiving and praise to him. And the greater my praise to him, the greater my love for him.

We need to know how sinful we are, but this teaching needs to be accompanied with the Biblical teaching that in Christ we are white as snow, and that there is no condemnation for those who are in Christ Jesus (Romans 8:1). If we accept Christ as Lord and Savior, then our sins are forgiven, covered by Christ's death on the Cross.

If you believe in Jesus Christ as your Savior, then you are as free from sin as if you have never sinned.

> Blessed is the one whose transgression is forgiven, whose sin is covered. Blessed is the man against whom the LORD counts no iniquity, and in whose spirit there is no deceit.
>
> Psalm 32:1-2

A further explanation of this Old Testament doctrine is found in 2 Corinthians,

> ...in Christ God was reconciling the world to himself, not counting their trespasses against them, and entrusting to us the message of reconciliation.
>
> 2 Corinthians 5:19

If we have been reconciled to God, then *in Christ* our trespasses are not counted against us. Our sins are not noted, for they are washed away by the blood of Christ. If you do not appreciate this, then you are not valuing the blood of Christ, and you are not valuing the redemptive power of the cross of Christ.

In order to accept the darkness and heaviness of our sins does not mean that we think of ourselves as without any worth or value. The Bible never says we have little or no value, in fact we have such great value that Christ died for us. We have so much value that he gave his own life for us. This makes us *his treasured possession*! (Exodus 19:5)

To sum up this whole line of argument: the more I am aware of the heinousness of my sin, the greater is my appreciation of the enormity of God's love. Why is it important that we realize how great our sin is? Not to make us feel "how terrible I am," No! But to help us understand how wonderful *he is*, and how valued we are by him.

Gracious God, help me to understand more fully the depth of my sin, and although I will never in this life fully understand the depth of my sin, I admit it to you now. And I accept your full forgiveness of all my sins, "though my sins be as scarlet, they shall be as white as snow" (Isaiah 1:18).

As a summary of this chapter, the words of Jesus on the Cross: "My God, My God, why have you forsaken me?" reveal to us the unimaginable pain that Christ experienced on the Cross. This was the great suffering that Christ experienced in order for our sins to be forgiven. He experienced separation from God. This is what we would have experienced if we had to bear the weight of our sins. So it is that the words "My God, My God, why have you forsaken me" reveal to us the quintessential center of the Gospel message.

After saying all this it is probable that I still think of myself as less guilty than I actually am. Maybe I think, *Yes, I have sinned, after all nobody is perfect, so I admit that I am not perfect, but I have not sinned so egregiously as to require Christ's death on the cross for the forgiveness of my sins.*

Did my sins require Christ to die a painful death on the cross? Were you there when they crucified my Lord? Yes, I was there. Not only was I there, I watched it.

Not only did I watch it.

I did it.

My Lord, forgive me.

After Jesus experienced the greatest pain that any one has ever experienced, we could understand if his faith wavered. His first words after experiencing this great suffering were, "I commend my spirit into your hands." Even after he experienced the incredible pain expressed by "lama lama sabachthani," he trusted in God.

In the words "My God My God why have you forsaken me," Jesus was telling us more about God than anything else he said about God. And here is that meaning. That God loved us so much that he gave himself for us, and suffered for us the most intense pain ever experienced by any being!!!

Jesus felt tremendous pain on the cross. He was so shocked he cried out "why have you forsaken me?" Our Lord, though he was forsaken of God, still pursued his Father's work – the work he came to do. His prayer, in the midst of this violent storm, rang out with cosmic thunder. His prayer was addressed to his Father, "My God, why have you forsaken me." He did not murmur or complain, like Job did when he asked why he was born (Job 3:1-3), or Jeremiah when he said "Cursed be the day on which I was born (Jeremiah 20:4)."

Notice also that, he did not leave the cross; he did not unloose the nails as he might have done with a command. He did not leap down amidst the assembled mockers, and scorn them in return, and chase them far away, but he kept on bleeding, suffering, even until he could say, "It is finished." Jesus did not say, Lord, get me down from this Cross, the pain is too great. No, he trusted God and he believed that God had a purpose for what he was permitting.

Our Lord did die on that cross. At the time he died, he had received no answer to his question of "Why?" His question went on ringing through heaven and earth. Our Lord died. And he was buried. And he spent three days in the grave. No answer came. For three days. On the third day God raised him from the dead, and then Jesus saw the answer to his question: "My God, why have you forsaken me?" For there, all along the golden streets stood a great number of the redeemed, singing praises to the Lamb, and this was a glorious answer to his question.

One of my biggest struggles personally is that my praise to God is often directly related to my feeling at the moment. If I am joyful and hopeful, why then, I am able to praise God enthusiastically. But if I am feeling dejected and dreary, then my ardor has cooled, and I am not so filled with praise. In fact it becomes difficult for me to sing with unrestrained praise! *Holy Spirit, I think my greatest need is to grow in faith so I can thank you cheerfully no matter what the horizon looks like. Holy Spirit, please help me to grow in this manner.*

And Walter, how do you think the Holy Spirit will teach you this lesson? The answer is, by giving you many opportunities to thank him by faith!

Do you think that the value of Christ's death on the Cross depends upon your feelings right now? How could it be that the efficacy of Christ's atoning death is related to how you are *feeling* at this moment? Could it be that the efficacy of Christ's death on the Cross is *independent* of anything about you??? Specially your inner feelings? Why not say to God, thank you for your death on the Cross, independently of how you are feeling right at this moment?

Christ experienced great anguish on the Cross, in part, to show me how much he loves me. I watch it and I do not see it. I do not fully grasp the enormity of it. I do not understand it. *Oh Lord, help me in my ignorance!! I do not understand the greatness of your love for me.*

If I did understand the greatness of Christ's sacrifice for me, I would have no doubt at all, *ever*, of the fact that all things work together for good to those who love God (Romans 8:28). I would believe totally in his abounding mercy for me. I would totally believe that his love would swamp my unbelief and my disobedience! If I do not fully believe this, then it is my fault! He has given me the evidence and the logic to convince me. If I am unconvinced, then it is *my doing*. It is my sinful decision not to believe in the face of the wonderful evidence that God has given to me. Lord, I confess my sin. Help me. Please deliver me from this sin.

Why do you allow me to have such little faith? In the light of the greatness of what Christ did for me on the Cross, why do you allow me to understand *so little* of this greatness? Anything more kind to me is grace, a gift, and mercy because he wills it, and he gives grace to whom he wills to give grace! But in asking this question I am asking God, why do you withhold your grace from me for a time, as if he has not the right to do this! In other words I am saying, why do you not let *me* be God, and let me make the decisions which only *you* have the prerogative to make?? Let me make the decision of when you will give me understanding. Lord, I accept that it is *your* decision. It is up to *you*! When and how and why, is all up to you.

So it is that the most important teaching in the Bible helps us to understand the infinite magnitude of God's love for each one of us. And our response to the most important teaching in the Bible will determine whether we spend an eternity with God or separated from God.

Is Christ's atonement the ultimate atonement, or could there be others? Christ is the ultimate and the only way of atonement!!! If there were a better way of atonement, then God would have selected that one!! But there is not a better one! For he already selected the best one!!!

Thank you Lord, for choosing the ultimate and the best way of atonement in Jesus Christ. Could God have forgiven us for our sins if Christ had not died on the Cross? Yes, because God can do whatever he wills to do, but this is how he chose to do it, so it must be the best way it could be done.

Christ's death on the Cross is God's best effort!! Are we to reject his best effort because we have a better way? There is no better way. There is no other best way.

The most important teaching in the Bible is: *Christ died for our sins.*

CHAPTER 3
An Explosive Expulsion of Exorbitant Praise

But I will hope continually, and will praise you yet
more and more.

Psalm 71:14

Lord God, I call you to the witness stand! Do you solemnly swear,
so help you God, to tell the truth, the whole truth and nothing
but the truth? I will question you now. Be pleased to answer me.

Here is the question. Have you behaved toward me in a manner
that deserves my personal praise? Once I have determined the answer
to this question, I will decide whether to praise you more and more.

There are many passages in Scripture which urge us to praise
you continually. But it may be, oh Lord, that you are not worthy
of my praise all of the time! It may be that you have taken actions
toward me which were not completely loving, which were not fair or
just. In this case I ask you to apologize to me, and to make amends

for your actions. And then I can consider the question of whether I will praise you more and more.

Horrors! I would never summon God to the stand and speak to him in such a fashion. But is this not exactly what we are doing when we refrain from praising him? Do we not refrain from praising him because we have decided that he is not deserving of our continual thanksgiving? We are told to praise him continually, yet we choose to abstain from this practice.

> Through him then let us continually offer up a sacrifice of praise to God,
>
> Hebrews 13:15

When we see the words "I will praise you more and more" (Psalm 71:14), it is not our calling to pass judgment on whether or not God is worthy of our praise. It is not our calling to evaluate God and determine whether he has behaved in the best manner possible, and then to decide that we will praise him because we approve of his behavior! It is our calling to praise God *continually*, at all times.

This is the best course I can pursue. I can go through life having decided in advance that I will praise him at all times for everything, because I believe he always behaves toward me in a manner that is deserving of my praise. If I have made this decision in advance, then whatever situation I encounter, I can draw upon this earlier commitment of mine, and proceed to "give thanks in all circumstances (1 Thessalonians 5:18)."

When Disaster Strikes!

What about when tragedy strikes? Why did God permit my father to die of cancer when I was fourteen years old? This question has been with me for seventy-one years. My dad had worked for the US State Department for thirty years. He loved his work, and was

37

admired and highly regarded as a diplomat. The summit for a Foreign Service diplomat is to become a United States ambassador to another country. My dad was the "acting ambassador" in Buenos Aires, Argentina in 1947. My dad had worked in Mexico for six years. He had been told by a superior who was a close friend that he was going to become US ambassador to Mexico upon the vacancy that was opening up there. But before that occurred, cancer took him in 1950. The day after he died, the main headline on the front page of the leading Mexican newspaper, the Excelsior, read: "HA MUERTO GRAN AMIGO DE MEXICO!" (A great friend of Mexico has died).

Why did my dad die at the peak of his career? I do not know. But I do know that God is good and merciful, and that I can praise him more and more. I loved my dad very much, and today, some seventy years later, I still have dreams each year about him. By faith I can give thanks to God that he is good and loving, even though I do not understand or like what transpired with regards to my father. There will be times in our life when we do not understand or like the things that are taking place in our world, but we can still bless God and praise him more and more. What do we when tragedy strikes? We praise him and bless his holy name. For he has not changed!

Avoid Swallowing Negative Emotions

I had a good relationship with my dad. I loved him and admired him greatly. I was fourteen when he died. It was a deep personal loss, and I did not have any experience in dealing with emotions of great pain and sorrow. A strange thing happened when I was thirty-four years old. I went to a three day conference designed to help ministers deal with the problems they face as they endeavor to help people. During this seminar there were some small group experiences where we were asked to share some of our deepest experiences in growing up. I talked about my father's struggle with cancer and his death. As

I talked about it in a clinical and analytical manner I found myself being inundated with feelings of sorrow and great pain. I began sobbing deeply. Soon I was crying uncontrollably. The people in my small group were empathic and supportive, and we spent the next hour talking about me and my father. This was the first long cry I had since my father died twenty years earlier. I received further counseling help from a professional therapist after this experience.

At the age of fourteen I did not know what to do with feelings of deep hurt, so what I did was to *swallow* those feelings. I learned 20 years later that swallowing our feelings is not helpful. Swallowing my feelings was an effort on my part to avoid feeling the pain of losing my father. The best thing that could have happened to me at the age of thirty-four is just what happened. I talked about my pain and experienced some of the deep hurt of my father's death.

As I said earlier, I still have questions about my father's death. I do not like that my father died when I was fourteen. Although I believe in the sovereignty of God, I do not believe that God "caused my father's death," but I do believe that God permitted it to happen. And I still believe that God is good and just in all that he does. And with God's help I will continue to seek to offer him the continual sacrifice of praise (Hebrews 13:15).

There is a difference between the message that you assign to emotions you are feeling and the feelings themselves. The feelings that I experienced in my father's death were of great pain and sorrow. This is what his death felt like to me. The message associated with these feelings may be: "God does not care about you and your father, God does not love you, God is not good." I do have the ability to accept this message or reject it in favor of what the Bible teaches about God's nature when tragedy strikes.

As a fourteen year old what I did was to reject the feelings of pain and sorrow, as I did not want to feel them. I figuratively swallowed them. But the problem is that when you swallow your feelings they are thrown into a stormy ocean, and they come back in the form of a whale that seeks to swallow you! What we need to do with feelings of hurt is not to swallow them, but to *experience* them. This is why counselling with an experienced therapist can be helpful. A good therapist can help us to talk about the incident, and process the negative feelings without swallowing them. This is what began to happen to me at the age of thirty-four when I talked about my father's death with the small group at the seminar.

If we become aware of negative emotions that could be interpreted as saying "God does not care about you," we can endeavor to bypass that message and go directly to the one unchanging factor, and that is the greatness and beauty of our Lord Jesus Christ. He is glorious and worthy of our praise, always!

When your feelings seem to be sending you a message about God which is contrary to what Scripture says about God, choose to believe what the Scriptures say about God. When you encounter an event which brings pain (death of a family member), you need to feel that pain, and not *swallow* it. By swallowing a feeling I mean: refusing to experience that negative emotion and pretending that particular hurt does not exist.

When Jesus was bearing our sins on the cross, the Father allowed Jesus to experience the pain of losing the Father's presence. And also in the Garden,

> And taking with him Peter and the two sons of Zebedee, he began to be sorrowful and troubled. Then he said to them, "My soul is very sorrowful, even to death...And going a little farther he fell on his face and prayed, saying, "My Father, if it be possible, let this cup pass from me; nevertheless, not as I will, but as you will."
>
> Matthew 27:37-39

God allowed Jesus to feel deep pain in the garden. The soul of Jesus was very sorrowful, even to death, because he knew that great pain was coming. God allowed Jesus to experience this pain. The hurt was appropriate. Jesus did not *swallow his feelings*, although he said he could have,

> Do you think that I cannot appeal to my Father, and he will at once send me more than twelve legions of angels? But how then should the Scriptures be fulfilled, that it must be so?"
>
> Matthew 26:53-54

Jesus could have avoided the pain of his suffering. He could have swallowed his feelings, but he knew it was in God's plan for him to experience this suffering, or else the Scriptures would not be fulfilled. In the same manner, there are emotional and physical sufferings that we need to experience in order to be fully human, and in order to understand Christ's sufferings.

What Is The Reason God Created Us?

This is a question which has been often discussed. An answer is found in Ephesians 1:1-19,

> To the praise of his glorious grace. Ephesians 1:6
> To the praise of his glory. Ephesians 1:12
> To the praise of his glory. Ephesians 1:14

We are to praise him for his glorious grace, for a decision made by God which occurred before the foundation of the world. It was a decision made by God the Father before we ever did anything. We did not yet exist! It was a decision made by God that was not dependent upon any action that we might take during our entire lifetime. It was not a decision made by God because he knew what we were going to decide! ("You did not choose me, but I chose you," John 15:16).

We are created in order to praise God. We are to praise him every moment of every day. We are to praise him in all situations. This passage in Psalm 71:14 – ("I will praise you yet more and more"), merits our meditation for long periods of time. We shall never exhaust its inner gold.

More and more. This means that today I can praise him more than I did yesterday. And tomorrow I can praise him more than I will praise him today. How can that be? Our logic tells us that since we are finite, our resources are also finite. So how can it be that I can praise him more and more? There is only one way that it can be possible, and that is if somehow I can be in touch with resources that are greater than my own finite resources.

I am!

I am in touch with the Holy Spirit, who will supply me with an unending amount of praise that I can give to my Lord. *Holy Spirit, do whatever you want to do in me so that you can supply me with ever increasing praise for me to pass on to my Lord.* So when I read Psalm 71:14, let my heart pray: "Lord, I want to praise you more and more."

Here is an excellent barometer for self-evaluation. If I am praising him more and more, than I can conclude that I am growing. If I am not praising him more and more, then there is a problem with my spiritual journey.

It is God's desire that we grow in our faith.

For this is the will of God, your sanctification.

1 Thessalonians 4:3

Look to him, and he will enable you to praise him more and more! The amount of praise that we have given God up to this point in time falls far short of his full due. Jesus died for *all* my sins, past present and future. None of us have yet expressed sufficient gratitude for the enormity of this gift. This is why we need to praise him more and more.

Just a couple of days ago I was thinking about the question "why praise God?" and I am embarrassed to admit what came to my mind. The first thing that came to my mind was: because the bible teaches we are to praise him, and because it is good for us. Then finally, I reread this chapter and it jumped at me with great force that we are to praise him because of the Atonement, because he died for us. I can never thank him enough for this.

Here is a good exercise for you: every moment you have a free pause in time to think whatever you want to think, praise him for dying on the cross for you. While you are walking to the dining room, watering the roses, walking down the fairway to hit your next shot in golf, brushing your teeth, taking a shower, or waiting for the water to boil.

The devil is feverishly at work to keep us from thinking favorably about the atonement, to keep us from thanking Christ for his death on the cross. With the help of the Holy Spirit, we can resist the flaming darts of the evil one (Ephesians 6:16-18) and continue to praise God in all circumstances for everything (Ephesians 5:20, 1 Thessalonians 5:18).

Are you praising God more and more? If you are not, then you are probably praising him less and less. It is a certain truth that if we do not go forward in the Christian life, we go backward. You cannot stand still; there is a drift one way or the other.

It will be in proportion as you hope for the good things which he has promised to your faith, that you will render to him the praise which is his royal revenue. *Every Christian as he grows in grace should have a loftier idea of God*. Our highest conception of God falls infinitely short of his glory, but a mature Christian enjoys a far clearer view of God than he had at the first.

It is God's desire that I praise him more and more. He tells me that! So when I pray that phrase in the Lord's Prayer, "Thy will be done", I am in fact asking that he bring me to the place of praising him more and more!!!

One of the greatest ways to progress in our Christian journey is this: no matter where you are, no matter what you are feeling, start to praise him more and more. And you will never know whether this really works or not unless you try it.

Is It Egocentric Of God To Desire That We Praise Him Continually?

The devil says, "Your God must be megalomaniacal, for he needs for the universe to circle around him, and for his people to make him always the center of attention. Why do you worship such a self-centered entity?" It seems like a valid question, but remember, Jesus said that the devil is "a liar and the father of lies" (John 8:44). The devil's position is that God desires our praise due to a weakness on his part. But this cannot be true, because God has no weakness. The Bible says that God is completely and totally good.

> The Rock, his work is perfect, for all his ways are justice. A God of faithfulness and without iniquity, just and upright is he.
>
> Deuteronomy 32:4

> This God—his way is perfect; the word of the Lord proves true; he is a shield for all those who take refuge in him.
>
> 2 Samuel 22:31

Since God is perfect in all his ways, his desire for us to praise him is not a weakness on his part, but it must be for our good. If God is pure goodness, then we can conclude that the reason we are to praise God is primarily for our own benefit! It is the best course of action for us to take in this life.

C.S. Lewis wrestles with this when he says:

> We all despise the man who demands continued assurance of his own virtue.[5]

After an incisive discussion of why we are to praise God, Lewis says "I think we delight to praise what we enjoy because the praise not merely expresses but completes the enjoyment; it is its appointed consummation."[6]

> Through him then let us continually offer up a sacrifice of praise to God, that is, the fruit of lips that acknowledge his name.
>
> Hebrews 13:15

> I will bless the LORD at all times; his praise shall continually be in my mouth.
>
> Psalm 34:1

It is not ours to arraign the Almighty, but to submit to him. We are not his censors, but his servants. It is not up to us to determine who God should be, or how he should behave. It is up to us to learn who he is. It is up to us to worship and praise the God who is described in the Holy Scriptures, rather than the God we create from our own imaginations and suppositions, and from our own ideas of what would be the ideal God. While there is much in the Scriptures that we do not understand, yet we are able to believe by faith that

---

[5] C.S. Lewis, *Reflections on the Psalms* (New York, Harcourt, Inc., 1958), 90

[6] Op. cit., For one of the best discussions I have seen on this subject see Lewis's chapter entitled: "A word About Praising," 90-98, Lewis concludes on the subject of praising God; "In commanding us to glorify him God God is inviting us to enjoy him." page 97.

God always speaks the truth. That which we cannot understand we nevertheless believe.

Shall We Praise Him Now Or Later?

Sometimes we say, *Well, I think I can begin to praise God continually when I have straightened things out in my own life.* Perhaps tomorrow I will have studied Scripture enough to understand God more fully, and then I can start praising him more and more. No! Start now!

> Praise, O servants of the LORD, praise the name of the LORD! Blessed be the name of the LORD *from this time forth* and forevermore! From the rising of the sun to its setting, the name of the LORD is to be praised!
>
> Psalm 113:1-3

There is nothing said in Psalm 113:1-3 about beginning to praise God after certain events have transpired. No. The Psalmist says to praise him now, *from this time forth and forevermore.* Praise him *now,* no matter what you are experiencing.

Shall I praise him only when my feelings are what I desire them to be? Or is it more important that I praise him *regardless* of what my feeling are? Whether I am praising him or not does not need to depend on any exterior circumstance, like my feelings, or health, or wealth, or my golf swing. It should depend only on the Biblical teaching that I am to be praising him always, at all times, *by faith.*

How can I praise God when it is not logical? There are many cases in the Bible where God gave a directive which seemed illogical. Jeremiah was told to buy an undesirable plot of land (Jeremiah 32:7-27). Paul and Silas were led to sing in jail (Acts 16:16-31). Moses was led to walk into the dead sea (Exodus 14:15-31). And yet these illogical orders were followed by great praise and singing.

The most important reason for us to praise God is because he committed the greatest act of good that has ever been done, when Christ died on the Cross for you and me, so that we would not have to pay the price for our own sins. *Christ's atoning death on the Cross is the greatest reason why we should praise him.* Christ's death on the Cross is the greatest, most important event ever to take place in the history of the world. Regardless of whatever evil or good is taking place in the world, the most important event of all time is Christ's death on the cross.

Stephen Hawking And My Free Will

Underlying the entire subject of this book is a very important question. Do I have free will?

Do I have the ability to decide that I will exercise faith in God's sovereignty and praise him at any time I choose to do so, even though my feelings and circumstances may be telling me that I am unable to do so.

When God promised to give his children manna in the desert, we are told it is important that they believe God will provide that manna. God is displeased when they murmur in disbelief.

> And the LORD spoke to Moses and to Aaron, saying, "How long Shall this wicked congregation grumble against me? I have heard the grumblings of the people of Israel, which they grumble against me.
>
> Numbers 14:26-27

> And without faith it is impossible to please him, for whoever would draw near to God must believe that he exists and that he rewards those who seek him.
>
> Hebrews 11:6

> Let us then with confidence draw near to the throne
> of grace, that we may receive mercy and find grace
> to help in time of need.
>
> Hebrews 4:16

As God wanted Israel to believe he was going to provide their daily manna, so God desires that we believe he is going to provide us with the unsearchable riches of Christ (Ephesians 1:7, 3:8). It is by our faith that we show God that we believe he is going to provide us with the riches of Christ. If we do not have free will, then it is not possible to exercise our faith, and thereby please God. "Without faith it is impossible to please God" (Hebrews 11:6). So it must be possible for us to show faith in God.

The question of whether we have free will is important because there are times when our circumstances seem so threatening that we think that we are not able to praise God and give him thanks. Some great thinkers have said we do not have free will. Stephen Hawking (one of the most famous physicists of the last hundred years) says, "... it seems we are no more than biological machines, and that free will is just an illusion,"[7] and he bases this conclusion on physics. Hawking adopts a thorough reductionist view, which says that there is nothing inside the human body other than particles whose behavior can be physically measured, such as electrons, protons, quarks, and that all these particles must follow the laws of physics. The behavior of the body is therefore determined by these particles and the laws of physics, with no part played by a "supposed free will." Hawking's position is true if in fact the body is composed only of "materially identifiable particles," but it is at this point that Hawking's theory can be questioned, for how would one prove that the human body is composed of nothing but measurable particles? The Bible teaches

---

[7] Stephen Hawking and Leonard Mlodinow, *The Grand Design* (New York: Bantam Books, 2010), p. 32

that there is an additional component in humans called spirit, and that this spirit can make free-will decisions. [8]

There is an interesting parallel here to modern particle physics. Since the 1920's, scientists have known that our universe is expanding, and they thought that it was expanding at a decreasing rate of speed. In the 1990's two teams of scientists set out to experimentally measure this cosmic expansion, and to the great surprise of the scientific world both teams found that our universe's expansion was not slowing down, but it was increasing in speed. There was no scientific explanation for this phenomenon. According to all the identified particles in our universe, the size of the universe should be expanding at a *decelerating* rate, since the gravitational pull of each star and galaxy on every other star and galaxy would be slowing down the cosmic expansion. Physicists have concluded that there must be some particles (given the names *dark matter* and *dark energy,* and unidentified as to this date) that cause cosmic expansion which is accelerating.[9]

If scientists were to follow Hawking's assumption that we do not have free will because of the reductionist model of the human body, then this kind of logic would lead us to conclude that the universe could not be accelerating at an increasing rate, because there are no known particles which produce this effect of repulsion on other particles. But scientists have not taken this approach because experimental data has shown that the universe *is* growing at an accelerating rate. How is this to be explained? Modern physics explains this by assuming that there is *something* in space which

---

[8] Many times in the Bible the word spirit refers to a human component of the body, such as Acts 7:59, Romans 1:9, 8:16, Galatians 6:18, Philippians 4:23, 2 Timothy 4:22, Philemon 25, James 2:26, 1 Peter 3:4

[9] For a discussion of this material on our expanding universe, see Brian Greene, *Until The End of Time,* (New York, Knopf, 2020), 253-255. Greene is a professor of physics at Columbia University. See also Sean Carrol, who is a Professor of Theoretical Physics at the California Institute of Technology, *The Big Picture,* (New York, Dutton, 2016), p. 183-185

they call *dark matter* and *dark energy* which have a repellant effect sufficient to bring about a cosmic expansion at an accelerating rate, even though dark matter and dark energy have not been identified or detected. This is analogous to saying that there is an "added component" to the body called our spirit, which can have the effect of exercising free will and thus influence the behavior of our body.

To say there is no such thing as free will would be analogous to saying that there can be no such thing as dark matter or dark energy. And we cannot say that there is no such thing as dark energy or dark matter because experiments have confirmed that the universe is expanding at an accelerating rate. These experiments showed that there is something that is causing an accelerating expansion of the universe whether we call it dark matter, or dark energy, or *the dark unknown*! This last statement assumes "scientific thinking," which says that every effect has a cause, i.e. if the universe is expanding at an increasing rate of speed, there is *something* that is causing this expansion at an increasing rate of speed.

All the above discussion is to show that it is logical and possible for us to say that we are able to exercise faith and praise God if we choose to do so. It seems significant to me that we had to search heaven and earth, and the very ends of the universe, and to plumb the depths of theoretical physics (as it has progressed to the present time) to show that a reductionist view of matter does not prove that there is no room for free will (as Hawkins argues).

I have the free will to believe that God's Hesed (steadfast love) is ever before me, right in front of my eyes.

> For your steadfast love is before my eyes, and I walk
> in your faithfulness.
>
> Psalm 26:3

His steadfast love is always situated right before my eyes, whether these eyes be open or closed. Why not open my eyes, and see his Hesed! Bathe in it. Experience it. Enjoy it. Benefit from it. It is there.

It is always there. All I need to do is believe that it is there. If I have no free will, then I am unable to open my eyes and see his Hesed. If I have no free will, then it is pointless for Scriptures to tell me that I can open my eyes and see his steadfast love right in front of me, waiting to engulf me.

By the grace of God, I can open my eyes and see.

But, says the skeptic within me, what if I open my eyes, and there is no steadfast love there? What if his Hesed has suddenly fled, leaving me with nothing but empty space to behold.

The Lord, whose word never fails, has promised that his Hesed never ceases, and is always before us. Open your eyes now, as you read these lines, and see his magnificent steadfast love waiting to enfold you.

> The steadfast love of the LORD never ceases; his mercies never come to an end;
>
> Lamentations 3:22

But what if sin has crept in and wedged its way in between me and God's steadfast love? No doubt sin has crept in, for it is ever working, but Christ's death on the cross has wiped us clean, white as snow.

> Come now, let us reason together, says the LORD: though your sins are like scarlet, they shall be as white as snow; though they are red like crimson, they shall become like wool.
>
> Isaiah 1:18

When we open our eyes, as long as we are looking through Christ on the cross, then we are carried directly and immediately to God's steadfast love. So, open your eyes now, and look with awe and wonder at the ever present, unfailing steadfast love of God. Open your eyes now, and see the Shepherd as he is described in Isaiah.

> He will tend his flock like a shepherd; he will gather
> the lambs in his arms; he will carry them in his
> bosom, and gently lead those that are with young.
>
> Isaiah 40:11

Open your eyes, and behold. It is important that you believe he is there waiting to bless you. Without faith, it is impossible to please God.

> And behold, I am with you always, to the end of
> the age."
>
> Matthew 28:20

A Brilliant Move When I Am In Deep Trouble

There are many situations in the Bible where an individual's situation appears to be mired in terrible conditions, yet amazing things can still happen as a result of faith. Let us look at such a case involving Jeremiah, when he ponders the trials he is experiencing.

> Remember my affliction and my wanderings,
> the wormwood and the gall! My soul continually
> remembers it and is bowed down within me. But
> this I call to mind, and therefore I have hope: The
> steadfast love of the LORD never ceases; his mercies
> never come to an end; they are new every morning;
> great is your faithfulness. "The LORD is my portion,"
> says my soul, "therefore I will hope in him."
>
> Lamentations 3:19-24

Jeremiah is a perfect example of trusting God by faith when things logically make no sense at all. When Jeremiah says in Lamentation 3:19 "Remember my affliction and my wanderings" he is referring to his own recollection of the trials he has experienced in Lamentations Chapters 1-3 and in Jeremiah Chapters 37 and 38. He was drowning in disasters. The Lord told Jeremiah to warn the people that those who stay in the city will die by the sword, but he who surrenders to the Chaldeans shall live. Jeremiah passed on to the people the message that the city will be given into the hand of the enemy. The officials of the king did not like the message that Jeremiah was proclaiming, and they went to the king and said to him,

> Let this man be put to death, for he is weakening the hands of the soldiers who are left in this city, and the hands of all the people, by speaking such words to them. For this man is not seeking the welfare of this people, but their harm... So they took Jeremiah and cast him into the cistern of Malchiah, the king's son, which was in the court of the guard, letting Jeremiah down by ropes. And there was no water in the cistern, but only mud, and Jeremiah sank in the mud.
>
> Jeremiah 38:4-6

Ebed-melech, a eunuch who was in the king's house, heard that they had put Jeremiah into the cistern. He went to the king and said:

> My lord the king, these men have done evil in all that they did to Jeremiah the prophet by casting him into the cistern, and he will die there of hunger, for there is no bread left in the city. Then the king commanded them to draw Jeremiah up from the cistern so that he would not die.
>
> Jeremiah 38:9-10

When Jeremiah said "The steadfast love of the Lord never ceases" in Lamentations 3:22, he was in the midst of great personal tragedy and pain. When Jeremiah pondered his afflictions and wanderings (Lamentations 3:19), this led him to deep despair, so that "my soul is bowed down within me (Lamentations 3:20)." In the midst of this despair, Jeremiah *made a brilliant move*! Jeremiah said: "But this I call to mind, therefore, I have hope (Lamentations 3:21)."

In the following verses (Lamentations 3:22-23) Jeremiah says what it is that he brought to mind. Jeremiah started to meditate upon the goodness and greatness of God, even though his circumstances had not changed. Jeremiah brought to his mind the following thoughts:

> The steadfast love of the LORD never ceases; his mercies never come to an end; they are new every morning; great is your faithfulness
>
> Lamentations 3:22-23

When Jeremiah started to meditate upon the steadfast love of the Lord, then he found that these great truths about God (Lamentations 3:22-23) pierced through his sadness and enveloped him in hope. It pleases God when we praise him independently of what our circumstances are at the moment. This is what Jeremiah does when he says that the steadfast love (Hesed) of the Lord never ceases and his mercies are new every morning. When Jeremiah makes his brilliant move and thinks of God's faithfulness, then he is filled with hope.

> "But this I call to mind, and therefore, I have hope.
>
> Lamentations 3:21

We can praise God and hope in God no matter what the circumstances.

> But I will hope continually,
> And will praise you yet more and more.

Psalm 71:14

Are There Any Situations That Legitimately Preclude Praising God?

Read through *all* the places in the Bible where it says we are to praise God, and you will not find *one* passage that has an "exception clause" in it. You will find no passage that says we are to praise God only if certain conditions do not exist alongside our present situation. The only conclusion we can draw from this is that *there are no circumstances which would preclude our praising of God.*

An exception clause would be:

a. We are to praise him, except when we are in jail.
b. We are to praise him except when the trees are all barren, with no fruit.
c. We are to praise him except when our body is riddled with painful sores.
d. We are to praise him except when a son or daughter is taken from us.

There are no passages in the Bible that tell us that we are *not* to praise God in any of the above four situations. But there is precisely the opposite situation in the Bible. There are passages in the Bible that tell us we *are* to praise God in the midst of these specific situations.

About midnight Paul and Silas were praying and
singing hymns to God, and the prisoners were
listening to them.

Acts 16:25.

Though the fig tree should not blossom, nor fruit be
on the vines...and there be no herd in the stalls...
Yet I will rejoice in the Lord, I will take joy in the
God of my salvation.

Habakkuk 3:17-18

Though he slay me, I will hope in him.

Job 13:15

Give thanks in all circumstances; for this is the will
of God in Christ Jesus for you...

1 Thessalonians 5:18

*There is no moment in which it would be right to suspend the
praises of God*: so let us offer the sacrifice of praise to God *continually*.
We bless the Lord as he is pleased to reveal himself, whatever that
revelation may be. Let us bless him by being totally satisfied with
anything and everything he does. When we do not understand his
ways, we can still praise and adore him. By faith. We choose to
submit our reason to faith. We cannot explain him rationally, but
we choose to adore him by faith, because he is always good, and he
always does what is just and right.

The purpose of his will was that we might be engaged in praising
him; that we might be to the praise of his glory, swimming in this
grace that was lavished upon us, so that we might offer him the
sacrifice of praise continually. God created us so that we might
praise him.

the people whom I formed for myself that they
might declare my praise.

Isaiah 43:21

It has not been the purpose of this chapter to give you an
intellectual basis for praising God at all times! The basis for praising
God is "by faith" in his command. So take this step now by faith,
that means without rational justification! That which is seen is not
faith! Take the step of faith *now*! I will praise God more and more
by faith!

The principle is this: No matter what is taking place in my life,
it is still my great privilege to praise God, for he is constant during
my turmoil. No matter what I see when I read the newspaper, God
is constant! He is still worthy of my praise.

The intensity of our praise should not depend on whether we
understand why he should be praised. It is better for the intensity of
our praise to be determined by our trust in the teaching of the Holy
Scriptures, rather than by our external circumstances. In this way
our faith is NOT dependent upon our circumstances, but our faith is
dependent upon the Word of God (Hebrews 13:8, Numbers 23:19).

Trust God For How And When Your Life Is Going To End

Normally when we praise God, we think of praising him for things
he has done to bless us in the past. But what about praising him for
things *he is going to do* on our behalf in the future. Paul told us to
give thanks for everything (past, present, and future),

giving thanks always and for everything to God the
Father in the name of our Lord Jesus Christ.

Ephesians 5:20

The "everything" includes the way that God has treated us in the past, and it also includes the things God is going to do in our lives in the future! I believe this activity on our part is something that brings pleasure to God for it shows him that we have faith in how he will treat us in the future. If we believe that he is going to treat us well in the future then let us thank him in advance, by faith. This faith is based upon the amazing promise found in Romans:

> And we know that for those who love God all things work together for good, for those who are called according to his purpose.
>
> Romans 8:28

If all things work together for good, then we can trust God that the time and manner of our death will work together for good. Many people worry about their future. They think about what their death will be like. Will it be sudden and unexpected? Will it be slow, and come after a time of suffering? Will my loved ones be by my bedside? We find the answer in Psalm 31:

> But I trust in you, O Lord;
> I say, "You are my God."
> My times are in your hand;
>
> Psalm 31:14-15

Thank God now for all the plans he has already made for your transition into the next life. Thank him now for the time of your death, the means of your death, who will be standing by your bedside, and any other questions you may have.

Can we praise God too much? No, we cannot. Because the words "more and more" in Psalm 71:14 stretch out to infinity. Once we have praised God "more" (the first more), there still remains the second "more." There still remains much activity of praise for us to be engaged in, for when we have praised him more, then we can engage in praising him *more and more.* When we have praised God with our very best effort, our praise is still as silence before God when compared with the praise that is due him from us. So let us raise the volume of our voices and praise him now enthusiastically, exuberantly, and bombastically, with more vitality and strength than we have in the past.

If we were to praise him with all the praise we can muster, it would still be less than his due!!! This means that if we were to praise him enthusiastically every moment, every second of all 24 hours of the day, every day of the week, every week of every year, it would not reach his due!!! Would it be too much praise? NO! It would not be enough!!! And yet here we are, wondering if at any moment of a normal day, there is a basis for me to praise God?

Loving Father help me to praise you at all times. Make whatever changes are necessary in me so that I will earnestly praise you at all times, for the present and the future, no matter what is taking place in the world or in my life at the time.

CHAPTER 4
God Wills What is Best for Me

The steadfast love of the LORD never ceases; his
mercies never come to an end;

Lamentation 3:22

When the final curtain on human life is drawn, all of God's
creatures will sing together in joyous amazement:

That which I doubted so frequently was true! *God
always did what was the best for me.* God always
behaved with steadfast love toward me!"

At that moment a new stanza of the Hallelujah Chorus may
well be launched in heaven! This new stanza will proclaim that
God always did the best, the wisest, the kindest, and the most
loving thing which he could have done to each and every one of
his children. We are overjoyed that this is so! This provides inner

strength and peace to each one of us in this life as we go through many fiery trials. We will not always understand how our present circumstance could be the best possible one for us, but we can choose to accept this Biblical teaching by faith. If some situation other than our present situation would actually be better for us, then that is where we would find ourselves!

God Always Deals With Us In Love (Hesed)

A clear statement of this principle is found in Jeremiah:

> I will make with them an everlasting covenant, that I will not turn away from doing good to them. And I will put the fear of me in their hearts, that they may not turn from me. I will rejoice in doing them good, and I will plant them in this land in faithfulness, with all my heart and all my soul.
>
> Jeremiah 32:40-41

One chapter earlier, in Jeremiah 31:31-33, the Lord says he will make a new covenant with the people of Israel, and then in Jeremiah 32:40-41 the Lord refers to this new covenant, saying that as a part of this covenant he "will not turn away from doing good to them" and that he will "rejoice in doing them good with all his heart and soul" (this means God will always do good to his followers, with all his heart and soul).

Here are more passages which describe how God deals with his people.

> The steadfast love (Hesed) of the LORD never ceases; his mercies never come to an end.
>
> Lamentations 3:22

Many are the sorrows of the wicked, but steadfast love (Hesed) surrounds the one who trusts in the LORD.

Psalm 32:10

He loves righteousness and justice; the earth is full of the steadfast love (Hesed) of the LORD.

Psalm 33:5

but the LORD takes pleasure in those who fear him, in those who hope in his steadfast love (Hesed).

Psalm 147:11

Have mercy on me, O God, according to your steadfast love (Hesed); according to your abundant mercy blot out my transgressions.

Psalm 51:1

Deal with your servant according to your steadfast love (Hesed), and teach me your statutes.

Psalm 119:124

Let your steadfast (Hesed) love come to me, O LORD, your salvation according to your promise;

Psalm 119:41

Turn to me and be gracious to me, as is your way with those who love your name.

Psalm 119:32

Have mercy on me, O God, according to your steadfast love (Hesed); according to your abundant mercy blot out my transgressions.

Psalm 51:1

But as for me, my prayer is to you, O LORD.
At an acceptable time, O God,
In the abundance of your steadfast love (Hesed)
answer me in your saving faithfulness.
according to your abundant mercy, turn to me.

Psalm 69:13

O Israel, hope in the LORD!
For with the LORD there is steadfast love (Hesed),
and with him is plentiful redemption

Psalm 130:7

Turn to me and be gracious to me, as is your way with those who love your name.

Psalm 119:132

The above passages say that God's dealings with his servants will be in accordance with the principle of "God's steadfast love (Hesed)." What a wonderful principle to have in mind when I think of how God deals with me. *God deals with me always in accord with his new covenant with me, his steadfast love to me, his promise to never turn away from doing good to me, His commitment to keep his promise with all his heart and soul.*

Being gracious toward us is God's way of dealing with his people (Psalm 119:32). He always deals with us in a manner which is filled with grace. God deals with us according to his steadfast love and according to his abundant mercy (Psalm 51:1). It is important to notice that the Hebrew word Hesed (English transliteration) in the English Standard Version and the Revised Standard Version is translated by *steadfast love.*

Hesed is an important theological term in the Old Testament, and is used over 350 times in the Old Testament. It is a fundamental characteristic of God's nature. It governs how God behaves toward his children. I can always depend upon God to behave toward me according to his steadfast love (hesed). There are times when even God's most trusted soldiers disbelieve this doctrine, as when Elijah asks God to take his life!

When Elijah Attempts Suicide!

God's will for us is always better than our will. To pick an example from the Bible, let us look at Elijah in 1 Kings 18. This great prophet of the Old Testament was God's instrument in an amazing feat. The prophets of Baal had been mocking the Lord God. Elijah stood facing 450 prophets of Baal who were threatening to kill him. Elijah called for God to send fire from heaven. The fire came. The prophets were destroyed by a display of God's power. Ahab told Jezebel, the wicked queen, what Elijah had done to the prophets. Jezebel was furious and sent a messenger to Elijah to tell him that by the next day she would have him killed. When Elijah heard this, he became very afraid, settled under a broom tree, and asked God to take his life.

> Ahab told Jezebel all that Elijah had done, and how he had killed all the prophets with the sword. Then Jezebel sent a messenger to Elijah, saying, "So may the gods do to me and more also, if I do not make your life as the life of one of them by this time tomorrow." Then he was afraid, and he arose and ran for his life and came to Beersheba, which belongs to Judah, and left his servant there. But he himself went a day's journey into the wilderness

and came and sat down under a broom tree. And he asked that he might die, saying, "It is enough; now, O Lord, take away my life, for I am no better than my fathers."

1 Kings 19:1-4

Elijah said to God, "take away my life." Elijah was so afraid that he asked God to take his life. God did not grant Elijah's prayer, but instead sent an angel who nursed Elijah back to health. This is an amazing instance of when God declined to answer a specific prayer of one of his saints. God had a better answer than what Elijah requested.

The Lord did what was best for Elijah. God did not take away his life, but instead *He gave him some more work to do.* Elijah had come to the broom tree afraid of Jezebel and depressed. He leaves the broom tree with confidence and new energy. He left with a new assignment, which was to call out Elisha to be his successor, and to denounce Ahab.

When I find myself in the midst of difficult and painful trials I frequently question the proposition that God wills our best. I ask, *why does God permit me to be in a situation which brings me such discomfort and pain?* Remember, had any other condition been better for you than the one in which you presently are, God would have put you there. You are put by him in the most suitable place. So then be content where you are ("for I have learned in whatever situation I am to be content" Philippians 4:11). *You cannot be in a situation that is better for you than your present situation.*

Joseph Was Wrongly Imprisoned For Life

From the earliest events in Scripture, we read about the principles governing God's behavior toward his children. When Joseph's brothers sold him to the Ishmaelites (Genesis 37:38), they intended evil for him. They were jealous of Joseph. Their envy began when they realized that their father loved Joseph more than any of his brothers. They sold Joseph to the Ishmaelites. Then Potiphar's wife accused Joseph of assaulting her, which led to Joseph being cast into prison for many years.

> But the LORD was with Joseph and showed him steadfast love (Hesed) and gave him favor in the sight of the keeper of the prison. And the keeper of the prison put Joseph in charge of all the prisoners who were in the prison. Whatever was done there, he was the one who did it. The keeper of the prison paid no attention to anything that was in Joseph's charge, because the LORD was with him. And whatever he did, the LORD made it succeed.
>
> Gen 39:21-23

Even when bad things happened to Joseph, God was with him and watched over him. God permitted Joseph's brothers to sell him to the Ishmaelites. God could have prevented this evil thing from happening. But instead God permitted the event to take place because God was planning to bring great good out of this. The story of Joseph is a great example of how God permits an unpleasant incident to come upon his children and then brings great good from it.

> Joseph said to his brothers: "As for you, you meant evil against me, but God meant it for good, to bring it about that many people should be kept alive, as they are today."
>
> Genesis 50:20

A famine that lasted seven years came upon Egypt. Jacob and all his people were desperate as they were out of food. It was in this situation that Joseph was now second in command of Egypt, and could provide ample food for Jacob and all his people. So it came to pass exactly as Joseph stated to his brothers: "You meant it for evil, but God meant it for good." God dealt with Joseph and his brothers according to God's steadfast love.

During this entire incident with Joseph, God is behaving with his children in accordance with his steadfast love (Hesed).

One of the greatest celebrations in the Old Testament comes when Moses and the people of Israel sing a song to praise God for delivering them from slavery in Egypt. Moses then states the principle governing God's behavior to Israel during this time.

> You have led in your steadfast love (Hesed) the people whom you have redeemed; you have guided them by your strength to your holy abode.
>
> Exodus 15:13

Through this entire process God led Israel according to his steadfast love (Hesed). Hesed is a term used at many key moments in the history of Israel. This term is also used to describe God when he gave the ten commandments to Moses.

> So Moses cut two tablets of stone like the first. And he rose early in the morning and went up on Mount Sinai, as the LORD had commanded him, and took in his hand two tablets of stone. The LORD descended in the cloud and stood with him there, and proclaimed the name of the LORD. The LORD passed before him and proclaimed, The LORD, the LORD, a God merciful and gracious, slow to anger, and abounding in steadfast love and faithfulness, keeping steadfast love (Hesed) for thousands, forgiving iniquity and transgression and sin.
>
> Exodus 34:4-7

The Bible points out several times that the dealings of God with Moses and Joseph and the children of Israel were carried out through the principle of hesed (steadfast love).

I Want To Be A Gershonite

There are times when we think that we belong in a more responsible position in life. We should be making more important decisions. We need to remember the Gershonites. They were selected by God for a particular function. They were assigned a particular service, and given specific functions by God. Their service was described as "bearing burdens."

> This is the service of the clans of the Gershonites,
> in serving and bearing burdens...
>
> Numbers 4:24

They camped behind the tabernacle on the west side of the Israelite camp (Number 3:23). They were in charge of the covering of the tent of meeting, the screen, the hangings for the surrounding court, and were responsible for the transporting of these furnishings when the Israelites moved (Numbers 4:24-28).

Ithamar the son of Aaron, was their overseer (Numbers 4:28). Moses gave them two wagons and four oxen to help them perform their duties (Numbers 7:7). Each Gershonite had a specific assignment from the Lord. This is similar to the New Testament, where Paul talks about the different gifts of the Spirit that are assigned to believers, and how the Holy Spirit chooses the allocation of these gifts ("All these are empowered by one and the same Spirit, who apportions to each one individually as he wills" 1 Corinthians 12:11).

Not only did the Lord appoint the one who was to bear the burden, but he also appointed the burden for each Gershonite to bear.

> All the service of the sons of the Gershonites shall
> be at the command of Aaron and his sons, in all
> that they are to carry and in all that they have to
> do. And you shall assign to their charge all that they
> are to carry.
>
> Numbers 4:27

They were not to choose for themselves what burden they would carry. They were simply to do what they were told. We may not like the span of time which we are given to serve. The Gershonites were told the specific amount of time they were to serve. There is no record in the Bible that any of the Gershonites complained that their burden was too heavy, or too light, or lasted for too long. They accepted the burden that was given to them.

Just as the Gershonites were told what their service was to be, so you and I are told what is our cross to bear. And our responsibility is to take that cross, and bear it.

> And he said to all, "If anyone would come after me,
> let him deny himself and take up his cross daily and
> follow me."
>
> Luke 9:23

Take up the cross that God has designed for you; your present situation is the best for you, it will do you the most good, and prove the most effective means of making you perfect in every good word and work to the glory of God. Let us believe that whatever he appoints is best. By the grace of God, let us believe that God wants what is best for us. Lord, help me to be a Gershonite, who willingly and cheerfully obeys Your calling.

We need the attitude which David exhibited in Psalm 103. His emphasis was on the good things God did. In the beginning of Psalm 103 David shows us how he searched for the positive. In everything which David thinks about God, there is something that is praiseworthy.

In this delightful Psalm, one notes how David finds situations to praise. There are desponding murmuring people who find reasons for complaining everywhere. But a man of David's spirit, on the contrary, takes the honey out of every flower, and praises God in connection with everything. In Psalm 103:1-4 there are many things which would have made others mourn, but these things call forth songs of praise from David.

For instance, David gives thanks to "him who forgives all your iniquity (Psalm 103:3)," where some would be forever complaining that they had sins and what a burden those sins were. But David sings of sin as pardoned. Some would be grumbling about their sicknesses, but David sang: "who heals all your diseases (Psalm 103:2)." Others would be fretting about the pits which they struggled with, but David says "who redeems your life from the pit, who crowns you with steadfast love and mercy (Psalm 103:4)." David did not dwell on those things which were painful, but enjoyed dwelling on the things for which he could praise God, as Paul taught many centuries later.

> Finally, brothers, whatever is true, whatever is honorable, whatever is just, whatever is pure, whatever is lovely, whatever is commendable, if there is any excellence, if there is anything worthy of praise, think about these things.
>
> Philippians 4:8

David was a good Gershonite in that he believed that his burdens were assigned and regulated by God.

The Day My Wife And I Could Have Died

About forty-five years ago, my wife Paula and I were backpacking in the High Sierras, spending several nights in a tent near Lake Ediza, a beautiful lake in the High Sierras. Lake Ediza is about ten miles from Mammoth Lakes. It is located at the base of the Minarets. Mt. Ritter was beckoning us (about thirteen thousand feet high). We went.

After about six hours of an exhausting climb we reached the top. We stayed on the summit about half an hour, enjoying the view. We could see the top part of Half Dome (in Yosemite Valley) about fifty miles away! We started back down. After about thirty minutes we were in a chute headed downward at a mild grade, except for an occasional steep step. We reached a step about three feet in length. The only way to proceed was to let yourself jump down to the next level. Another step. Then another. And another. The steps seemed to be getting bigger. We stopped a while and had a serious discussion.

We came to the frightening conclusion that this was not the path we had taken to come up the mountain, because we did not remember climbing up any four foot high steps! We realized that we could not get back up to try and find the right way down, because by then we were too tired to try to make it back up. And there was no way to climb back up all these four foot high steps! Without realizing it, we were already committed, although not knowing what was ahead. Were there more four-foot steps? Did the steps ahead get longer than four feet? We were beginning to be afraid. We prayed. Lord, help! We could not go back, so we moved forward. Another four-foot jump. We could not see any clear path ahead, and we just kept going. After hiking down another fifteen minutes or so, the chute ended. It headed into empty space with a free-fall of over two hundred feet. We could not go that way. It would lead to a calamitous fall resulting in serious injury, or death.

Now I was really afraid. To our right was a solid wall. Straight ahead was the steep fall of over two hundred feet. Directly in back of us was a climb back to the top of the mountain, but we had already decided this was not a possibility. To the left was about a six-inch ledge which curved around a steep wall for about ten feet. Picture a nearly vertical wall with a ledge of six-inch width running across the face of it. We could see that this ledge went for about ten feet and then the almost vertical wall that this ledge traversed became less steep and you could jump off the ledge onto a surface that was almost flat.

A slip on that ledge would have meant falling over two hundred feet onto almost vertical rock. We prayed again. Lord do we go on, or not? We went. We walked slowly and carefully on to the ledge, one behind the other.

We held hands—if one fell, both would fall!

As you can tell, we made it. Thank You, Lord. On this little journey, our Lord overruled many of our bad decisions.

I think this was the most frightened I have ever been in my whole life. If we fell, would we survive, and if we survived would it be with some serious quality of life injuries? Earlier in my life I had studied Romans 8:28, and had determined "Yes, with God's help I will accept this teaching of the Bible for my life," but I never had thought I would experience such a severe test of my faith as to have to step on to that six inch ledge! (This was somewhat similar to an experience John Muir had during the first ascent ever recorded by anyone of Mt. Ritter in 1872.[10])

---

[10] 10 Muir, John, *The Mountains of California.* (Garden City, NY: Anchor Books, Doubleday and Company, Inc., 1961), 64-65. John Muir made the first ascent of Ritter Mountain in October 1872. Muir describes a perilous section of his ascent: 'I was suddenly brought to a dead stop, with arms outspread, clinging close to the face of the rock, unable to move hand or foot either up or down. My doom appeared fixed. I must fall. There would be a moment of bewilderment, and then a lifeless rumble down the one general precipice to the glacier below. When this final danger flashed upon me, I became nerve-shaken for the first time since setting foot on the mountain, and my mind seemed to fill with a stifling smoke. But ... life blazed forth again with preternatural clearness. I seemed suddenly to become possessed of a new sense. ... Then my trembling muscles became firm again, every rift and flaw in the rock was seen as through a microscope, and my limbs moved with a positiveness and precision with which I seemed to have nothing at all to do. Had I been borne aloft upon wings,

What if we had not made it back safely? What if one or both of us had died? We realize in looking back that we might not have returned. There have been people in similar situations who did not make it back. That could have happened to us! Well, if we had not made it back in good health, I could still believe the Biblical teaching that our lives were in the Lord's hands. I would have many unanswered questions, but with God's help and by his grace I could still believe that God is always working good for us. Yes, this would be a powerful challenge to my faith, but not as powerful as the challenge to Jesus' faith when he found himself on the Cross, with his question to the Father unanswered (My God, why...?).

Why is it so difficult for me to believe that God always does what is best for me? It boils down to ONE ISSUE! God has promised to behave toward me according to his steadfast love. Either I believe It or I do not. Which will it be for you?

Tell him now.

Lord, I would not change one thing which you have done in my life!! Everything you did in my life was the absolute best!! The highest!! I can trust you with leading me in the best possible manner. There is not one single time when you led me in a way that was not the best possibility for me. Oh Holy Spirit, grant me the faith to believe this with all my heart.

It would require an infinite mount of wisdom to know what is always the best course of action for me. Indeed, this would require omniscience! Fortunately for us, God *is* omniscient. But we are not. In fact, God knows what is inside an electron! There is not a scientist alive today who knows what is inside an electron. It is a mystery to science. But God knows! And God knows what is the most desirable course of action for us in any situation. This is why Jesus taught his disciples to pray daily "your will be done" ("Our Father in heaven,

---

my deliverance could not have been more complete. ... I found a way without effort, and soon stood upon the topmost crag in the blessed light.'10

hallowed be your name…your will be done, on earth as it is in heaven. Give us this day our daily bread"…Matthew 6:7).

God also knows the exact number of stars in the entire universe and what is their name.

> Lift up your eyes on high and see: who created these? He who brings out their host by number, calling them all by name; by the greatness of his might and because he is strong in power, not one is missing.
>
> Isaiah 40:26

He is omniscient, and it is with that omniscience that God knows what is best for us, and that he knows how to always do what is best for us!! Jesus tells us that we will be frequently tempted to disobey God, and that we are to seek God's will.

I could pray that God might always deal with me in accordance with *my own desires*, but the problem with this prayer is that I would get it wrong a large portion of the time! What I end up asking for would not be nearly as good for me as what God's steadfast love would bring about. Jesus told us that we would be better off praying for his will, and not our will. (Matt 26:39 "…not as I will, but as you will.")

PRAYER: By the grace of God, and with the help of the Holy Spirit, may I always believe that You, Oh Lord, will do what is best for me.

CHAPTER 5
Irrationally Exuberant Love

"Behold, I have engraved you on the palms of my hands."

Isaiah 49:16.

I have before me at this moment a silver cup. It is about the size of a healthy grapefruit. It has some letters written on it. If you pass your finger over the letters you will know that these letters are carved into the silver cup, they are not simply written with a felt pen. The letters are "W A L T E R R A Y." That is my name. The cup also has engraved onto it:

"III TORNEO JUVENIL NACIONAL, FINALISTA, 2ᴬ CATEGORIA,"

which means Third National Tournament, Finalist, Second Category. At the age of sixteen, I had just graduated from the American High

School in Mexico City, and had entered a golf tournament for all boys sixteen and under in the entire country of Mexico. I finished in second place. I have had this cup for sixty-eight years, and it is one of my prized possessions.

The Engraving On A Cup

The carving on the cup assures that the name which is engraved on the cup will last for the lifetime of the cup. It has lasted sixty-eight years so far! It is permanently fixed upon the cup, and cannot be removed without significantly altering and damaging the cup itself. In like manner, the carving on the palms of my Savior Jesus Christ will endure for the entire existence of the Savior. Once I have been carved on the palms of his hands, that engraving cannot be removed. He will not remove it, and he will not permit anyone else to remove it.

> "Behold, I have engraved you on the palms of my hands."
>
> Isaiah 49:16.

The carving on the cup assures the person whose name is carved onto the cup that this person will always be worthy of the honor and blessings given to the recipient of the award of the cup. This person is the one to whom this cup has been awarded! It is a permanent action.

I can step out of my office and leave the cup on my desk. The cup and the engraved letters of my name will be far from me, and out of my sight, and probably out of my mind. But if the words are engraved on the palm of my hands, when I step out of the office, I cannot leave the palms of my hands on the desk. I must take my hand with me into the hallway and out of my room, so that I will always have the person represented by the engraved letters near at hand.

Imagine a church in Rio De Janeiro, Brazil, which has two hundred members. So Christ is involved with each one of these two hundred members, because they are engraved upon the palms of his hands. He is involved with their concerns, their daily problems and challenges, and with each member's thoughts about their families, their work, and their health. They are praying to him frequently during the day, he is listening to their prayers, and he is responding to their requests. During all our Lord's involvement with these two hundred members, *they are engraved upon the palms of his hands.* So not for an instant have any of his children vanished from his mind and his thoughts. They are always before him, in his mind and his thoughts. This means, dear beloved child of God, that our Lord is always with you and me, and has our wellbeing on his mind. This is what he said in Matthew 28:20, "Lo, I am with you always."

As The Nails Are Hammered, Our Name Is Engraved.

I believe we may take these words as spoken by Jesus Christ, and addressed to all who confess him as Lord and Savior. We may see him as dying for us on the cross. *As the nails are being hammered into his hands, we may see our own name being engraved onto the palms of his hands.* Let us borrow from the writer of Hebrews his line of reasoning when he says

> For to which of the angels did God ever say, "You are my Son, today I have begotten you"?
>
> Hebrews 1:5

To which of the angels did Jesus ever say: "Behold I have engraved you upon the palms of my hands?" None. Does this mean that we are worth more than the angels? It surely does suggest that we are more precious to Jesus than the angels are, since Jesus never said that the name of any angel was inscribed on the palm of his hand. Are we really? All the residents of heaven must have wondered in amazement that Jesus chose poor, human sinners above all other created beings.

In fact Jesus not only chose humans, but he chose humans who had just questioned God's own faithfulness and loyalty.

> But Zion said, "The LORD has forsaken me; my Lord has forgotten me." Can a woman forget her nursing child, that she should have no compassion on the son of her womb? Even these may forget, yet I will not forget you. Behold, I have engraved you on the palms of my hands.
>
> Isaiah 49:14-16

The Lord has comforted his people when they were afflicted and needy, and their response is to question his faithfulness and say "the Lord has forsaken me." After the Lord's people say "My Lord has forsaken me," the Lord says to them "Can a woman forget her nursing child? Behold I have engraved you on the palms of my hands." When a person has questioned your word and your reliability, it is difficult to express your own enduring love for them, and yet this is precisely what Jesus does when he says to us "I have engraved you on the palms of my hands."

It is the greatest marvel of all, that even when we provoke God with such unbelief, he is still faithful to a faithless people. We question him frequently. Every time we express a doubt in his wisdom, every time we murmur why did he not leave us in Egypt where at least we had garlic and leeks, we are grumbling about his sovereignty. Why did he not do it this way, instead of that way? Why did he not let me have my will, instead of his will? And his response is loving, gracious and merciful. "Behold, I have engraved you on the palms of my hands."

He keeps his promise to us a thousand times, yet at the next trial we doubt him once again! Will he keep his promise to me one more time? Can I trust him to lead me wisely once again? He never fails us. He is never as the setting sun whose light has diminished for the night. And yet we are troubled with anxieties, as if God were not totally dependable. It is amazing that after proving himself true to his promises to us, we doubt him again, and then again, and then one more time. Until Jesus says, "o ye of little faith." (Matthew 14:31)

His response to us is grace, and then more grace ("He gives more grace" James 4:6). His response is to say to each of us, "I have engraved you upon the palms of my hands." It is indeed a marvel that God repays our unbelief with grace.

Do we have any awareness of how sinful we are? So often we stumble along, seeking our own will. The Psalm writer expressed it well:

> But as for me, my feet had almost stumbled, my steps had nearly slipped. For I was envious of the arrogant when I saw the prosperity of the wicked.
>
> Psalm 73:2-3

> When my soul was embittered, when I was pricked in heart, I was brutish and ignorant; I was like a beast toward you.
>
> Psalm 73:21-22.

There are those times when we are jealous of our friends and their prosperity (Psalm 73:3). *I wish I could afford a house like theirs. I wish we could take vacations to those nice places where they go.* And when we are envious of the prosperity of the wicked, our feet sometimes stumble. These times we are brutish and ignorant (Psalm 73:21-22) and we are like a beast before God. So we admit that we are still sinful. But the truth is, we are a thousand times more sinful than we realize!! One of the great marvels is that in spite of our sin, he showers his love upon us ("Now the law came in to increase the trespass, but where sin increased, grace abounded all the more," Romans 5:20).

Who Can Write Upon The Hand of Christ?

No one can write upon the palm of God's hand except for God himself. Jesus said "You did not choose me, but I chose you." We did not decide to write our names upon the palms of God's hands. Only God could make the decision to write our name upon the palm of his hand. Not our merits, our prayers, and our faith, could write our names there. Nor could we suddenly have appeared on God's palms by blind chance or a fortuitous combination of circumstances. Only the intentional and omnipotent love of God's own heart could write the names of his people upon his own hands.

Isaiah 49:16 says "I have engraved *you*." Isaiah 49:16 does not say, "your name". It does not say I have engraved the letters of your name on the palms of my hands. It says "YOU." The name is there, but that is not all. The letters of your name are there, but there is more. "I have engraved *you*." I have engraved your thoughts, your emotions, your ideas, your consciousness, your subconsciousness, your heart, your body, your being, your identity, everything about you.

I have shared earlier how I struggle with my emotions when they are not what I desire them to be, when they are somewhat subdued, when they are less than I yearn for them to be, and when I cannot understand how they vacillate so freely. And yet, these very emotions which cause me such agonies and wrestling are engraved upon his palms. He is aware of them from the beginning of time. He is not surprised by them, and none of them can occur within my heart without his permission! Well then, why question them so repeatedly? Why do I not simply rest in the knowledge that he is aware of my condition, and that *any situation which he allows is the best possible situation in which I could find myself*? Well then, my Lord, I will praise you, more and more!!! Lord, then it is true that you can never ignore me, or forget me, for I am engraved upon the palms of your hands.

It is a custom among some to tie a string around their wrist or a finger in order to help them remember a particular matter of importance. Now a string may be broken, or snapped away, and so the matter might be forgotten, but the hand and that which is engraved upon it is constantly present. Remember, child of God, that by night and by day God is always thinking about you. From the morning of the day to the evening of that day, the Lord's eye is upon you.

> A pleasant vineyard, sing of it! I, the LORD, am its keeper; every moment I water it. Lest anyone punish it, I keep it night and day;
>
> Isaiah 27:2-3

The Lord takes care of his plants, every moment he waters them, and he keeps them day and night. The Lord's eye is upon you every moment. He takes care of you day and night.

Our thoughts about God are on and off. God's thoughts about us are never on and off. Although we pledge to praise him continually ("Let us continually offer up a sacrifice of praise to God" Hebrews 13:15), we find it difficult to keep our thoughts on him. But God keeps his mind continually upon us, for we are engraved upon the palms of his hands.

How do we try and explain this manner of maintaining remembrance by cutting it into his palms? He could have said "Shall I carve my people upon precious stones such as a ruby or a diamond?" No, for all these must disappear in time. Shall I engrave my people on silver and gold? No. For these too will pass away in time. I will write instead on myself, on the palms of my hand, so that my people will know that I will never forget them.

As if to say, "Behold, I am doing what is best for you, I am thinking about you all the time, I will never stop doing good to you." God is immutable, he will always maintain his love toward us, for has he not said that it is an everlasting love. When God saw the rainbow he said it reminded him of his everlasting covenant ("When the bow is in the clouds, I will see it and remember the everlasting covenant between God and every living creature of all flesh that is on the earth." Genesis 9:16). If seeing a rainbow can bring such a remembrance to the Lord, how much more can seeing our name imprinted on his own palms?

Do not judge the Lord by your outward circumstances.

> Now hope that is seen is not hope. For who hopes
> for what he sees? But if we hope for what we do not
> see, we wait for it with patience.
>
> Romans 8:23-25

Do not trust him only when you see what he is doing. Do not believe in him only when you can figure out everything he is doing and why. Trust him even when you can see no evidence of his goodness to you, for hope that is seen is not hope. Let us hope when we do not see.

How easily we say "all is against me" when things are not going our way (Genesis 42:36). In reality even when it appears that things are against me, God is at work bringing about his providential plan. He is at work doing good to me, and working all things together for good.

When we think that God has forsaken us, there is still involved a measure of God's grace. It was after Jehovah comforted his people that Zion said "Jehovah hath forsaken me, and my Lord hath forgotten me." Zion did not say this until God had visited her. That Zion realized she was without God's comfort was a result of God's grace, for otherwise Zion had not even been aware that she was laboring without a fuller measure of God's presence. Beloved child of God if you are aware of being deep down in the dungeon, be thankful that you want to get out of it. So there is a longing after

God, is there not? This is a working of the Holy Spirit in your soul, for he has made you aware that there is more, and that you can move closer to infinity. The presence of your initials on the palms of his hands are the guarantee that he is bringing you toward his infinite self.

There is, therefore, some trace of his hand in your spirit, even now that you say, "Jehovah hath forsaken me, and my Lord hath forgotten me." Every time I am aware of feeling some distance from the lord, it is a blessing because it will move me to desire his presence!!!!

He has said to each of us, I have done that which will render it utterly impossible that I should ever forget one of my people. I the Lord have committed myself to something which will henceforth render it absolutely certain that I never can forget my own, for *I have engraved you upon the palms of my hands.*

These words seem to say to us that God has already secured, beyond any possible hazard, his tender memory towards all his own. He has done this in such a way that forgetfulness can never occur at any moment whatsoever. The memorial is not set up in heaven, for then you might conceive that God could descend, and leave that memorial. It is not set up in any great public place in the universe, nor is it engraved in a signet ring upon God's finger, for that might be taken off. It is not written upon the Almighty's skirts, to speak after the manner of men, for he might disrobe himself for conflict; but he has put the token of his love where it cannot be laid aside, on the palms of his hands.

If he has put something, by way of memorial, upon the walls of his house or the gates of his home, he may go away, and forget it. Or if he shall write the memorial upon some precious diamond, or topaz, or other jewels which he wears, yet he might lay them on one side. But God says, "I have engraved you upon the palms of my hands," so that the memorial is constantly with him; yea, it is upon God himself that the memorial of his people is fixed.

No doubt a part of the wonder which is concentrated in the word "Behold" (Isaiah 49:16) is excited by the unbelieving lamentation of the preceding sentence. Zion said, "The Lord hath forsaken me, and my God hath forgotten me." How amazed the divine mind seems to be at this wicked unbelief of man!

What can be more astounding than the unfounded doubts and fears of God's favored people. He seems to say, "How can I have forgotten you, when I have engraved you upon the palms of my hands? How can it be? How dare you doubt my constant remembrance, when the memorial is set upon my very flesh?" O unbelief, how strange a marvel you are!

Which should arouse the most wonder in us, the faithfulness of God or the unbelief of his people. He keeps his promise a thousand times, and yet one new trial makes us doubt him. He never fails us, and yet we are as continually vexed with anxieties, molested with suspicions, and disturbed with fears, as if our God were fickle and untrue. Here follows the great marvel, that God should be faithful to such a faithless people, and that when he is provoked with their doubting, he nevertheless remains true.

Be ashamed and confounded for all your cruel doubts of your indulgent Lord. The "Behold" in our text is intended to attract particular attention. There is something here worthy of being studied. If you should spend a month over such a text as this, you should only begin to understand it. It is a gold mine; there are nuggets upon the surface, but there is richer gold for one who can dig deep.

One of Hollywood's favorite themes is the love story. Someone falls in love with desperate longings, with a love so strong that it transcends all surrounding circumstances. It lifts you above suffering, illness, poverty, oppression and depression. It translates you into a world of glimmering ecstasy and unsurpassed emotional intensity. It will be a surprise to many people to find out that this is precisely the most salient story in the Bible. It is a love story where God says to you: I love you with all my heart and soul, and I am working on your behalf with all my heart and soul. Let us look once again at the words in Jeremiah 32:41,

> I will rejoice in doing them good, and I will plant them in this land in faithfulness, *with all my heart and all my soul* [emphasis added].

Nowhere else in the Bible are the words "with all my heart and soul" used to describe God's attitude toward anything. Is there anywhere else in all the Bible where it portrays God as saying that he feels so strongly about anything or anyone? No. Only in Jeremiah 32:41.

Many times a worker applies himself to a task with just enough energy to get the job done. But when a worker hurls himself into his task with all the energy he has, fortunate indeed is the recipient of his work. God has put himself into the task of raising his vineyard with all his energy and dedication. God has created the universe, the sun and the stars. God designed the plants, the flowers, the animals. He sculptured the mountains, the Everests and the Matterhorns, and the Grand Canyons. And out of all this magnificent creation, we are the greatest. Only of us does the Bible say that God dedicated himself with all his heart and soul. He will design us, he will place us in a vineyard of his own choosing, and all this to be done with all his heart and soul. For our joy, for our rejoicing.

He will plant us. Planting is often mentioned in the Scriptures. Why is the love story so important to Hollywood? Because it resonates with the strongest human emotions. It describes the most powerful emotions that any human being can experience. To set up the situation where a human can feel the most powerful emotions is to describe a situation where the reader is immediately drawn into the story, for they have been looking for this situation in their own lives.

Is it possible that God might have omitted one needful feature from the composition and design of his creatures? How can we know what is meant by the whole heart and the whole soul of the

Almighty? Yet all this is involved when the Lord blesses his people, whom he hath redeemed unto himself. He says it himself. Is there any other reference in the Scriptures where God says, speaking of himself, "with my whole heart and soul?" Only in Jeremiah 32:41.

No, it cannot be. It must be a fairy tale. It could not be true! But he did say "My thoughts are not your thoughts, my ways are above your ways, as is the heaven above the earth!!" (Isaiah 55:9) Yes, it is true. Dwell on it. Accept it! Think about it. Thank God for it.

Well then, why did I get that pain in my kidney yesterday? Why did my computer indicator on the dashboard show that one of my tires is low and needs filling? Why are we allowed to struggle with Covid-19? I do not know why. But I believe that God loves me and tends to every aspect of my life with "all his heart and soul."

With all his heart and soul!!! Believe him. Praise God for these words. Accept them as pure truth, as solid gold. But what if I cannot rationally understand them as I place them beside all my present circumstances?? Never mind whether I can understand God's actions. The Bible tells us that God's understanding is beyond measuring (Psalm 147:5). God's actions are beyond our understanding, so I will do better to accept His actions by faith, and not insist on trying to understand them with the logic of my own finite brain. He did not create us so that we would fully understand him. He created us so that we might have enough faith to give him thanks for all things, whether we understand them or not.

It is not possible for God to love us more than he already does. It is possible for us to praise him more and more, but *it is not possible for God to love us more and more.* He already loves us with all his heart and soul. He cannot love us more. He already loves us with every resource he has, he already loves us with all the strength and might at his disposal. He cannot love us any more.

He loves his son with all his heart and soul. When the prodigal son returned to his father's house the father is so overjoyed that he poured out his love on his son. Although his son had been selfish and had sinned grievously against the father by leaving him, the father poured out his love. The son came back to his father. But while he was still a long way off, his father saw him and loved him, and ran and embraced him and kissed him. What great unconditional love. Before the son even had the opportunity to apologize and confess, the father ran to him, embraced him and kissed him. The father did not keep back anything. The Father loved him with all his heart and soul.

> 'Bring quickly the best robe, and put it on him, and put a ring on his hand, and shoes on his feet. And bring the fattened calf and kill it, and let us eat and celebrate. For this my son was dead, and is alive again; he was lost, and is found.' And they began to celebrate.
>
> Luke 15:22-24

When a person has questioned your word and your reliability it is difficult to express your own enduring love for them. And yet this is precisely what Jesus does when he says to us "I have engraved you on the palms of my hands." We question him frequently. Every time we express a doubt in his wisdom, every time we murmur, *why did he not leave us in Egypt where at least we had garlic and leeks* we are grumbling about his sovereignty. *Why did he not do it this way, instead of that way? Why did he not let me have my will, instead of his will?* And his response is loving, gracious and merciful.

The next time you doubt God's work in your life remember the might and the strength God demonstrated while engraving you on the hands of Christ.

"Behold, I have engraved you on the palms of my hands."

CHAPTER 6
The Throne of Grace

Let us then with confidence draw near to the throne of grace, that we may receive mercy and find grace to help in time of need.

Hebrews 4:16

One of the most endearing and powerful, examples of grace ever depicted in literature is found in "Les Miserables" by Victor Hugo. Jean Valjean is an ex-convict with no job, and nowhere to go. He is given a free room for the night by a bishop. Jean Valjean steals some silverware, beating the bishop in the process, and leaves the next morning. The police catch him, and take him back to the bishop. Jean Valjean tells the policeman that the bishop gave him the silver. This was, in fact untrue, for Jean Valjean had stolen the silver. The Bishop told the police that he had given Jean Valjean the silver, where upon the police release Jean Valjean. This was an outrageous act of grace, for the bishop knew that Valjean had stolen the silver, yet tells the police that he gave the silver to Valjean. This act of grace on the bishop's part had a profound effect upon the life of Valjean.[11]

This kind of undeserved gift is what the Bible is suggesting in Hebrews 4:16 "Let us then with confidence draw near to the throne of grace, that we may receive mercy and find grace to help in time of need."

Whenever we are in a time of need God is ready to pour out great and unexpected grace upon us. He takes it from the full reservoir of grace within Jesus Christ, and lavishes it upon us. Are you in need of any grace from God at this moment in your life?

Grace Is More Than We Think It Can Be

Here is a family of Scriptures that deal with grace. As you read these passages may the Holy Spirit enable you to believe that God is working at this very moment to bring more grace into your life, seeking to bring about what he desires. If you will carefully study the Scriptures on grace that are listed here, you will come up with this most amazing characteristic of God's grace: God's grace is always more than we think it can be, and God's grace is always more than we deserve.

> And the Word became flesh and dwelt among us, and we have seen his glory, glory as of the only Son from the Father, full of grace and truth.
>
> John 1:14

> For from his fullness, we have all received, grace upon grace.
>
> John 1:16

---

[11] Victor Hugo, *Les Miserables*, (New York, Fawcett Publications, 1961) pp. 37-39

But the free gift is not like the trespass. For if many died through one man's trespass, much more have the grace of God and the free gift by the grace of that one man Jesus Christ abounded for many

Romans 5:15

So too at the present time there is a remnant, chosen by grace. But if it is by grace, it is no longer on the basis of works; otherwise grace would no longer be grace.

Romans 11:6

...according to the riches of his grace, which he lavished upon us

Ephesians 1:7

But he gives more grace.

James 4:6

May grace and peace be multiplied to you in the knowledge of God and of Jesus our Lord

2 Peter 1:2

The Biblical teaching is that God desires for every believer to grow in grace. It is God's will that that we receive more and more grace!!

But grow in the grace and knowledge of our Lord and Savior Jesus Christ. To him be the glory both now and to the day of eternity. Amen.

2 Peter 3:18

Rather, speaking the truth in love, we are to grow up in every way into him who is the head, into Christ,

Ephesians 4:15

It is important for us to realize that God desires for us to grow in grace. It is not a matter of our having to persuade God to allow us to grow in grace. *He desires* our growth in grace. It is his will that we grow in grace. So it is a matter of applying the means that he has set before us in the Scriptures for us to grow in grace.

Grace is always opposed by sin. Sin is powerful, but grace is more powerful!

Now the law came in to increase the trespass, but where sin increased, grace abounded all the more

Romans 5:20

Paul makes it sound like the *Fall* (the entrance of sin through the disobedience of Adam and Eve) has resulted in an increased abounding of grace. How could this be? It is God's mystery of grace, grace abounding, and grace which dwarfs the sin which caused the need of God's grace in the first place!

God is more glorified in the redemption of man than if there had never been a Fall. This does not mean that God caused the Fall in order to bring more glory to himself. Humans bear the responsibility of the Fall, but in God's sovereignty he brings greater good out of the Fall then would have existed without the Fall. If God had not taken an action in Christ to overcome the Fall then the Fall would have triumphed and there would have been no redemption which overcame the Fall. It may be that God himself knows a joy which he would not have known had there been no sin. This may seem a preposterous statement. But what else could it mean when we read "where sin increased, grace abounded all the more (Romans 5:20)."

There are times when we are sailing above our circumstances and our tendency is to become conceited from the flush of "good times." At these times it may be that God permits a thorn in our flesh to keep us humble, to put us in a position where we need his grace to rescue and strengthen us. Such times are permitted for our own good and for our growth, as Paul writes:

> So to keep me from becoming conceited because of the surpassing greatness of the revelations, a thorn was given me in the flesh, a messenger of Satan to harass me, to keep me from becoming conceited. Three times I pleaded with the Lord about this, that it should leave me. But he said to me, "My grace is sufficient for you, for my power is made perfect in weakness." Therefore I will boast all the more gladly of my weaknesses, so that the power of Christ may rest upon me. For the sake of Christ, then, I am content with weaknesses, insults, hardships, persecutions, and calamities. For when I am weak, then I am strong.
>
> 2 Corinthians 12:7-10

God is waiting for us to approach him with an urgent plea for grace. If your reply is, "I don't need more grace as I already have enough," then you have just shown that you are naked, and poor, and miserable, though you think yourself to be rich and increased in goods (Revelation 3:17). Grace leads us to gratitude. Grace never leads us to lift up ourselves and say, "I have done well to obtain it." Grace, like the cargo in the vessel, makes the ship sink deeper in the stream. You may measure your rising in grace by your sinking in humility.

The Lord will give nothing to you who claim it as a right, but he will give generously to those who come to him, admitting that they have no claim to his mercy, and pleading desperately that it may be bestowed upon them through the riches of grace in Christ Jesus.

What Determines The Amount of Grace I Receive?

There are times when I wish that I had received more grace than what I have actually received. The other day I wrote the following in my diary, May 22, 2021:

> Lord, anything good that I have is from You. It is a gift. Forgive me Lord for what I am going to write next, but why do I not have the amount of understanding of Scripture that you have given to Spurgeon? Why have you not given to me the gifts that you have given to Spurgeon[12] as far as the understanding of Your grace and goodness? Lord, I confess this sin! Yes, I admit it. I admit my sin of envy. Cleanse me from this sin, Oh God. Wash me white as snow from this crimson sin. Walter, spend more time thanking God for the of grace that you *do* have right now, rather than thinking about the grace that you do not have.

> Walter, remember that God's scale of grace is infinite. No matter how much grace you have been given, there will always be more grace that you have not yet fully received. This is one of the problems with infinite grace. You will not receive all of it, for there is always more. Be thankful that

---

[12] Many have called Charles Haddon Spurgeon "The Prince of Preachers." A well know German theologian, Helmut Thielecke, once made a statement about Spurgeon that is quite well known, and has often been quoted. In a lecture to seminary students, Thielecke said: "Sell all that you have and go buy Spurgeon."

God is infinite and you are not! Is this not Lucifer's primordial sin, that he wanted to be like God (Isaiah 14:14). My envy of someone else having more grace than I have, is like my wanting to be God!!! I would like to determine how much grace I receive! But the Biblical teaching is that it is up to God to dispense the amount of grace that he chooses for me! It is not up to me to tell God how much grace he is to give me. Lord, help me to totally accept the amount of grace that you select for me.

I yearn for the life of faith which believes that God will do great things! How blessed to go through our lives believing that he gives me more grace and leads me on from height to height, that he enlarges my capacity, and helps me to feel that he will give me a greater capacity yet to receive. Yes, he gives more grace. More and more.

As we journey through our daily adventures we may find ourselves thinking that our journey might have been smoother if only God had done this or that or the other.

After all, even Albert Einstein made a mistake in his calculations. In 1917 Einstein introduced to his equations a term he called "the cosmological constant." Many years later he called this his "greatest blunder."[13] Even the brightest scientific mind, like Einstein, may have made an error in his equations. But when it comes to God's influence on our lives and the distribution of God's grace upon us, God has never, and will never, make an error in his decisions!

It is not possible for God to make any kind of mistake in the amount of grace he bestows upon us, and in the manner in which he bestows his grace upon us. If only I could truly believe this with all my heart as I go through my daily life, what great peace and joy

---

[13] Isaacson, Walter. *Einstein; His Life and Universe*, (New York, Simon & Schuster, 2007), 353-356

this could give to my easily troubled heart. Help me, Oh Holy Spirit, to believe more wholeheartedly in this grace of my Father.

> Now may the God of peace who brought again from the dead our Lord Jesus, the great shepherd of the sheep, by the blood of the eternal covenant, equip you with everything good that you may do his will, working in us that which is pleasing in his sight, through Jesus Christ, to whom be glory forever and ever. Amen.
>
> Hebrews 13:20-21

"Working in us that which is pleasing in his sight." God is always working in us that which is pleasing in his sight. How can I become certain of that? It is written in his Word. The writer of Hebrews assures us that God has enough power to "work in us that which is pleasing in his sight," for he refers to him as "the God who brought again from the dead our Lord Jesus." (Heb 13:20-21). If God is working in me that which is "pleasing in his sight" then God is working to give me precisely the amount of grace that is the best for me. He decides!

Wait a minute, I have a problem, I cannot praise God any more now, because I have just exhausted my supply of praise! Nonsense, you will never exhaust your supply of praise! It is God's will that we praise him at all times, continually (Hebrews 13:15). The word for "grow in grace" in the Greek of 2 Peter 3:18 ("But grow in the grace and knowledge of our Lord and Savior Jesus Christ") is a verb in the imperative tense. This means that it is a command. Peter is commanding the believers to "grow in grace." You and I are directed as believers to grow in grace. To grow in grace and in the knowledge of Jesus Christ is not optional. It is a mandate for every believer. God will never run out of resources with which to meet our needs, for his supply comes from: "his riches in glory in Christ Jesus" (Philippians 4:19).

Yesterday my cup of grace was full. But today it is empty and I need a refill. Yesterday the Israelites were praising God for getting them through the dead sea with the Egyptians hot in pursuit, but today they were murmuring and wishing that they had the good old "leeks and onions" instead of the manna (Numbers 11:5).

Last night when I went to bed, I was feeling his goodness, but now, I am feeling discouraged and dejected. The truth is, I will never have accomplished enough to maintain yesterday's grace. I always need a fresh supply. I will never have kept myself far enough from sin so that I merit today's grace. I have not been good enough to merit fresh grace for today. I have not praised him enough, I have not shown him sufficient faith. I do not deserve his grace. But do not therefore give up, Walter. Ask him and believe him for fresh grace for right now, and for today! And he gives it right now, because he chooses to. Because he wants to. Because he wills to. Doesn't all this make for a perfect definition of grace?

Or would you rather have the definition be: grace is what I *deserve* and have earned by my faithful obedience to Scripture!!

It is by grace,
>   And it is a gift,
>>   A gift of God,
>>>   A gift which God desires for us to have!

The Difference Between Grace And Works.

If I start thinking "I have done well to be at my present level of grace," then beware: for I am thinking of grace in terms of "works," as a benefit bestowed upon me for something I have done! In which case it is not a gift at all, but it is a wage paid in exchange for good works.

If I am totally honest with myself, sometimes I feel like praying:

> Oh Lord, I will praise me more and more, for look
> how humble I am, how believing I am, how much I
> trust You!! Oh, how good of me to praise You more
> and more!!!"

But if I am thinking along these lines, then grace is something I have brought about by my own efforts, by my own good works, whereas the Bible teaches that you can do nothing to earn God's grace. There is nothing you can give God in exchange for his grace. You will never be able to do anything in order to deserve his grace. There is only ONE way you may receive his grace, and that is as an outright gift from God, brought on through your faith in Jesus Christ.

> For by grace you have been saved through faith.
> And this is not your own doing; it is the gift of God,
> not a result of works, so that no one may boast"
>
> Ephesians 2:8-9

> Now may the God of peace who brought again
> from the dead our Lord Jesus, the great shepherd
> of the sheep, by the blood of the eternal covenant,
> equip you with everything good that you may do
> his will, working in us that which is pleasing in
> his sight, through Jesus Christ, to whom be glory
> forever and ever.
>
> Hebrews 13:20-21

The God of peace is the one who is working in us that which is pleasing in his sight. This is an important teaching, for if I think that *I* work in me that which is well pleasing in his sight, then this is *works*, not grace. But it is God who works in me – this is grace, not works!!!

Grace comes by God's decision and by his action. Remember, I have done nothing to *deserve* salvation in Christ. It is an outright gift. It is a pure act of grace on God's part. You may measure how much you have risen in grace by noting how far you have sunk in humility. So it is written about Jesus that when he emptied himself, he grew in humility.

> Have this mind among yourselves, which is yours in Christ Jesus, who, though he was in the form of God, did not count equality with God a thing to be grasped, but emptied himself, by taking the form of a servant, being born in the likeness of men. And being found in human form, he humbled himself by becoming obedient to the point of death, even death on a cross.
>
> Philippians 2:5-8

God's grace is great goodness since it visits persons so insignificant, so guilty and so deserving of wrath. Blessed be God that he is good to persons so ungrateful, to persons who cannot even at the best make any adequate return, who, alas, do not even make such return as they could.

If you believe that you have received a great amount of grace, that is good, but do not stop now. There is much more. You are just beginning this amazing journey. You are simply touching the hem of his garment. The life of faith believes that God will do great things.

We are often tempted to give partial credit to grace, and partial credit to works. We say, *Well of course salvation is by the grace of God, but then, I must add my own obedience to his will, my good works. NO!* It is *all* grace, it is not mostly grace plus a small amount of good works by me! But if this is the case, then are we not saying good works are unimportant, and we can do whatever we want to do? No, we are not saying that good works are unimportant. If we have been justified by faith in Christ then we have been given a new heart and we will desire to do good works. The desire to obey his will shall be written on our hearts, as he has given us new hearts (Jeremiah 31:33). Good works are important, but when it comes to recording the source of our salvation, it is not "grace plus good works." It is grace. Could Paul have said it any more forcefully than this?

> …chosen by grace. But if it is by grace, it is no longer on the basis of works; otherwise grace would no longer be grace. (Romans 11:6)

More than that, she who trusts in herself, her feelings, her works, her prayers, or in anything except the grace of God, *virtually gives up trusting in the grace of God altogether.* God's grace will never share the work with our merit. As oil will not combine with water, so neither will human merit and heavenly mercy mix together. The apostle said,

> If by grace, then it is no more of works: otherwise grace is no more grace. But if it be of works, then is it no more grace: otherwise work is no more work."
>
> Romans 11:6

You must either have salvation wholly because you deserve it, or wholly because God graciously bestows it though you do not deserve it. You must receive salvation at the Lord's hand either as payment of a debt or as a charity. There can be no mingling of the ideas. That which is a pure donation of favor cannot also be a reward of personal merit. A combination of the two principles of law and grace is utterly impossible. Trust in our own works in any degree effectually shuts us out from all hope of salvation by grace; and so it frustrates the grace of God.

It is easy to fall into the trap of believing that grace is a gift, but that there are certain spiritual laws which I need to follow in order to be eligible to receive and maintain this grace. But in stating it this way I have now placed grace in the category of works. Look again at Ephesians 2:8-9,

> "For by grace you have been saved through faith.
> And this is not your own doing; it is the gift of God,
> not a result of works, so that no one may boast."

Grace is not of your own doing. Grace is not of works. If it is my own doing and the result of something I have done, then it is works.

Is It Just To Receive Grace If I Do Not Deserve It?

Grace is inextricably related to the sovereignty of God. The Lord reigns. He does whatever he pleases to do (Psalm 135:6). Since he is the ultimate power, he can do whatever he chooses to do. Is it just for me to receive gifts from God if I do not deserve them?

Do you really want what you *deserve* from God? What you and I deserve from God is: separation from God! "The soul who sins shall die," Ezekiel 18:4, "All have sinned and fall short of the glory of God," Romans 3:23. We have, everyone of us, sinned and fallen short of the glory of God. So what we justly deserve is death. Thanks be to God that he does not give us what we deserve.

> He does not deal with us according to our sins, nor
> repay us according to our iniquities. For as high
> as the heavens are above the earth, so great is his
> steadfast love toward those who fear him;
>
> Psalms 103:10-11

It is very difficult for us to accept that we have no rights before God. It is hard to accept that God can truly do whatever he pleases, and that he owes us nothing. Oh, how this infuriates us! Who is God to say this? Well, as a matter of fact, he *is* God and he does whatever he pleases!

> What shall we say then? Is there injustice on God's part? By no means! For he says to Moses, "I will have mercy on whom I have mercy, and I will have compassion on whom I have compassion." So then it depends not on human will or exertion, but on God, who has mercy...You will say to me then, "Why does he still find fault? For who can resist his will?" But who are you, O man, to answer back to God? Will what is molded say to its molder, "Why have you made me like this?"
>
> Romans 9:14-20

Grace through Jesus Christ is the pathway to God. But I do not want to accept the Biblical teaching that what I justly deserve from God is death. After all, I have my rights! But the problem is: if we come to God seeking our rights, we will get nothing. If we come to God confessing that we have no rights, we will receive everything.

The reason for God's grace to me is not anything that I have done. It is purely an act of God, and the reason for it is in his heart. I will most likely not know the reason for it in this lifetime, other than that it is due to his love.

The Lord does whatever he pleases. My role in this is to accept whatever he does as being just and good.

> "For you are a people holy to the LORD your God. The LORD your God has chosen you to be a people for his treasured possession, out of all the peoples who are on the face of the earth. It was not because

you were more in number than any other people that the LORD set his love on you and chose you, for you were the fewest of all peoples, but it is because the LORD loves you and is keeping the oath that he swore to your fathers, that the LORD has brought you out with a mighty hand and redeemed you from the house of slavery, from the hand of Pharaoh king of Egypt.

Deuteronomy 7:6-9

The Lord can do anything he desires. There is nothing He owes me. The Lord says to you, "May I not do as I will with my own?" He will give nothing to you who claim it as a right, but he will give everything to those who come to him confessing that they have no right to his mercy, and pleading that it may be bestowed upon them through the riches of his grace in Christ Jesus.

I am the LORD your God, who brought you up out of the land of Egypt. Open your mouth wide, and I will fill it But my people did not listen to my voice; Israel would not submit to me.

Psalm 81:10-11

The lord wanted to bless Israel, and told them to open their mouths wide. But they would not submit to him, because the blessing did not come in the form that they wanted it. So they did not listen to him. When we pray to God and ask for help, we need to submit our will to his will, and we need to accept his answer in the manner which it comes. If we say "But Lord, this is not the answer I wanted," then we are asking for our will rather than his will.

Jacob is a prime example of someone who does not deserve God's mercy. Through deceit, and by lying to Isaac his father, Jacob stole Esau's birthright. When Esau comes to Isaac to receive his father's blessing, Isaac then realizes that Jacob deceived him by presenting himself to his father Isaac as Esau, and Isaac says to Esau:

> "Your brother came deceitfully, and he has taken away your blessing." Esau said, "Is he not rightly named Jacob? For he has cheated me these two times. He took away my birthright, and behold, now he has taken away my blessing."
>
> Genesis 27:35-36

Esau hated Jacob and said:

> Now Esau hated Jacob because of the blessing with which his father had blessed him, and Esau said to himself, "The days of mourning for my father are approaching; then I will kill my brother Jacob."
>
> Genesis 27:41

Jacob heard that Esau was planning to kill him, and went to God in prayer, asking God to protect him from his brother's wrath. Jacob was not yet ready to confess his sin to Esau, but he was more than ready to ask God to help him. Jacob prayed,

> I am not worthy of the least of all the deeds of steadfast love and all the faithfulness that you have shown to your servant, for with only my staff I crossed this Jordan, and now I have become two camps. Please deliver me from the hand of my brother, from the hand of Esau, for I fear him, that he may come and attack me, the mothers with the children. But you said, 'I will surely do you good, and make your offspring as the sand of the sea, which cannot be numbered for multitude.'
>
> Genesis 32:10-12

Notice two important features of Jacob's prayer. First, Jacob approached God with humility, for he knew that he did not deserve God's help to protect him from Esau. He showed his humility when he approached God with the words "I am not worthy of the least of all the deeds of steadfast love (Hesed) and all the faithfulness that you have shown to your servant" (Genesis 32:10).

Secondly, he reminded God of his promise when he said "But you said, I will surely do you good..." (Genesis 32:12). One of the strongest elements of any prayer we make to God is to claim a promise that God has made to us.

This is a good lesson from Jacob. We are to approach God in humility when we pray, for we never *deserve* any kind of good answer from God. Any answer that God gives to us is purely by his grace and his goodness. Yes, it is just to receive grace if I do not deserve it, because God can decide what to do with his riches. Remember, Jesus said of the laborers in the vineyard:

> Am I not allowed to do what I choose with what belongs to me? Or do you begrudge my generosity?
>
> Matthew 20:15

How Do We Receive God's Grace?

We have spent this chapter looking at God's grace and the Biblical teaching that "he gives more grace." How do we actually receive more of this grace? What procedure will make it ours? The steps are actually quite simple (so that a child could receive grace). We find this procedure delineated in the following passage in Ephesians 3:16-21:

> That according to the riches of his glory he may grant you to be strengthened with power through his Spirit in your inner being, so that Christ may

dwell in your hearts through faith—that you, being rooted and grounded in love, may have strength to comprehend with all the saints what is the breadth and length and height and depth, and to know the love of Christ that surpasses knowledge, that you may be filled with all the fullness of God. Now to him who is able to do far more abundantly than all that we ask or think, according to the power at work within us, to him be glory in the church and in Christ Jesus throughout all generations, forever and ever. Amen.

The procedure outlined above is that you receive God's grace by faith. You will then have strength to comprehend and understand the breadth, length, height and depth of the grace you are receiving, thereby enabling you to be filled with all the fullness of God. The way to comprehend and understand the grace you are receiving is to study it in Scripture, meditate upon it, think about it, affirm it. *During your meditation*, "The God of our Lord Jesus Christ, the Father of glory, will give you the Spirit of wisdom and revelation... having the eyes of your heart enlightened, that you may know what is the hope to which he has called you, what are the riches of his glorious inheritance in the saints, and what is the immeasurable greatness of his power toward us who believe (Ephesians 1:17-19)."

Here is a practice which will bring you great grace. "We have thought on your steadfast love (Hesed), O God, in the midst of your temple" (Psalm 48:9). The practice of thinking on his steadfast love is essential in order to be a mature Christian. We need to think in harmony with the great thoughts of God, thinking them over and over again, endeavoring not to think of anything contrary to what is revealed about God in Scripture. If we are to grow in grace and to advance in the Christian life, we are to read, ponder, meditate upon, and assimilate the amazing truths taught in Scripture about God.

The steadfast love of God is a Scriptural theme that is specially worthy of our thought. No one can say about the steadfast love of God, "I have thought the subject dry, I have picked it clean and exhausted its fulness." This is a theme not only worthy of thought, but beyond all thought. Thank God for his steadfast love which has given us Christ to be our intercessor, and whose prevailing prayers are continually before God on our behalf.

Some people like to think about their troubles, and dwell on them over and over, again, and again, and again until they make themselves as miserable as a human being can be. Some people are never content until they are dissatisfied. Some people like to analyze the members of their church, harping on their faults and failings. Would it not be better to think and talk about the steadfast love of the Lord?

David said "My heart became hot within me. As I mused, the fire burned; then I spoke with my tongue (Psalm 39:4)." As we think and meditate (muse) upon the steadfast love of the Lord, the fire and the zeal burn within us. It is good to think about the steadfast love of the Lord, and to meditate upon all his wonderful attributes, for as we do so our faith will grow.

Remember, it is not by your own strength and initiative that you will win God's grace.

> for not by their own sword did they win the land,
> nor did their own arm save them, but your right
> hand and your arm, and the light of your face, for
> you delighted in them.
>
> Psalm 44:3

> For not in my bow do I trust, nor can my sword
> save me. But you have saved us from our foes and
> have put to shame those who hate us. In God we

have boasted continually, and we will give thanks
to your name forever.

Psalm 44:6-8

If you ask me why the Lord is willing to pour grace upon his people, we can find no answer in them or their deserving, but the psalmist gives us the reason Christ thus acts in faithfulness and tenderness. "He leadeth me in the paths of righteousness *for his name's sake*" (Psalm 23:3). He would not restore us for our sakes. There is nothing in us which could be pointed out to the eye of justice as a claim for restoration, though much might be remembered which, on the footing of the law, would ensure our ruin.

The Lord Jesus has willed to save us, and he stands to his purpose and decree; he has put forward his own veracity and immutability as guarantees of the covenant, and his own honor would be in jeopardy should one of his people be lost, therefore for his own name's sake he restores the wanderer, lest his enemies should say, "God has forsaken his people," and lest the hosts of hell should boast, saying, "The Lord began to save them, but he was not able to finish the work." "For his name's sake." What a glorious reason. *For his name's sake* he pours his grace upon us.

When we see some people who overflow in grace, remember that they do not have a monopoly on grace. Whatever grace the best have had, you may have as much and more. Do not imagine, my beloved friends, that the standard of your attainment is the maximum of a Christian. Do not consider that you have obtained all that God is willing to bestow. There are loftier degrees of sanctification, there is a more eminent nearness of communion than the most of us have. The laid-up treasures in the Holy Spirit are vastly greater than any of us have ever been able to conceive.

There is nothing which God will give to some of his people which he will not give to all his people. There is not one of those who feared and trusted him that was worthy of the least grain of his mercy. They were many of them the chief of sinners, and yet this great goodness, came to them, exemplifying its greatness because of the greatness of their transgressions. Was there any worthiness about the prodigal who had devoured his substance with harlots in his riotous living?

When God saved Jonah by the whale which was prepared for him, did he do it because Jonah was deserving of it? Far from it. He was fleeing from God's presence and the path of duty, and God's goodness to him is in bold opposition to Jonah's disobedience. Well may we say, as we notice our own waywardness and folly, and contrast it with the divine mercy, "Oh, how great is your goodness, Oh Lord!"

> But he gives more grace... God opposes the proud
> but gives grace to the humble.
>
> James 4:6

He never means less than he says, but he always means more than we think he says. For this let us magnify the Lord. His power to bless us is not limited by our ability to understand the blessing. Grace is not measured to us according to our capacity to receive, but according to his efficacy to bestow. How do we receive God's grace? By faith, and in humility.

His power to bless is not dependent upon what he sees when he looks deep inside us. For when the Lord looks inside us he sees Jesus Christ. He sees us "in Christ," for we are "in Christ" (the phrase "in Christ" occurs about ninety times in Paul's letters).

> Blessed be the God and Father of our Lord Jesus
> Christ, who has blessed us in Christ with every
> spiritual blessing in the heavenly places, even as he
> chose us in him before the foundation of the world,
> that we should be holy and blameless before him.
>
> Ephesians 1:3-4

Paul is saying that when God sees us in Christ, he sees us as holy and blameless. This is also how he sees us as part of the church: holy and blameless.

> as Christ loved the church and gave himself up for her, that he might sanctify her, having cleansed her by the washing of water with the word, so that he might present the church to himself in splendor, without spot or wrinkle or any such thing, that she might be holy and without blemish.
>
> Ephesians 5:25-27

If when God looks inside of me he sees me as "holy and blameless," then I surely can brush aside any objections on my part such as: "But I am not worthy of receiving his grace." If he sees me as holy and blameless and, if when he looks inside me he sees Jesus Christ, then I am more than worthy of receiving his grace (but not by my own merits)!

How can I know whether I am receiving God's grace or not? Not by how I feel. But by faith. By faith in the teachings of Scripture I can accept that God is bestowing grace upon me at all times, even right now at this very moment!

> Let us then with confidence draw near to the throne of grace, that we may receive mercy and find grace to help in time of need.
>
> Hebrews 4:16

CHAPTER 7
Is Racism A Sin?

But in humility count others more significant than yourselves.

Philippians 2:3

Why include a chapter on racism in a book about spiritual formation? Because if we truly desire to grow in our relationship with Jesus Christ, then we need to make an effort to oppose the practice of sin in our own lives, and the Bible teaches that racism is a sin.

The Two Greatest Sins In The Bible

In the Gospel of Mark we find that Jesus named two great commandments.

> And one of the scribes came up and heard them disputing with one another, and seeing that he answered them well, asked him, "Which commandment is the most important of all?" Jesus answered, "The most important is, 'Hear, O Israel: The Lord our God, the Lord is one. And you shall love the Lord your God with all your heart and with all your soul and with all your mind and with all your strength.' The second is this: 'You shall love your neighbor as yourself.' There is no other commandment greater than these."
>
> Mark 12:28-31

Jesus not only named two great commandments, but he said these two were the greatest commandments. "There is no other commandment greater than these." Love God with all your heart, and love your neighbor as yourself. We sin when we break either one of these commandments: We sin when we do not love God, and we sin when we do not love our neighbor.

One of the most powerful definitions of not loving our neighbor is found in Philippians:

> Do nothing from selfish ambition or conceit, but in humility count others more significant than yourselves.
>
> Philippians 2:3

This bring us to an issue which looms large in the world today: racism. Here is the definition of racism in the Oxford dictionary:

"The inability or refusal to recognize the rights, needs, dignity, or value of people of particular races or geographical origins. More widely, the devaluation of various traits of character or intelligence as 'typical' of particular peoples."

Whenever I think of someone else as "less significant than myself" because of their race, this is "racism." This is in direct violation of Philippians 2:3. There is no way around this by use of sophistry, or intellectual arguments of any kind. Jesus taught that the second greatest commandment is to love our neighbor as ourselves. This means we are to accept them as they are and value them as highly as we value ourselves, in fact value them *more highly* than we value ourselves (Philippians 2:3).

The USA has been guilty of racism for four hundred years!!! Black Americans have been asked to use different rest rooms. Black American have been forbidden to eat meals in the same dining areas as white Americans. Black Americans have been asked to use different rest room facilities than white Americans. Black Americans have been forbidden to drink from the same water fountains as white Americans. Black Americans have been forbidden to swim in the same swimming pools as white Americans. Black Americans have not been permitted to sleep in the same hotels as white Americans. Black Americans were not permitted to sit in the same part of buses as white Americans. Black Americans were not permitted to serve as heads of Fortune 500 companies. Black Americans were not permitted to play on Major League Baseball Teams. Black Americans were not permitted to play in the highest-ranking golf tournaments.

Yes, it is true that many of the above parameters have changed, and while in many instances an overt racism has been eliminated, many scars remain, and sadly, many of these racist conditions still exist in some parts of our country. Well into the twentieth-century lynching was held before audiences sometimes in the thousands. Some schools would let out early so that white children could watch these murderous sadistic acts performed on black people. Racism was deeply embedded into many parts of our society.[14]

I Will Follow The Lord And Do What I Want

Present day examples of unbalanced treatment between blacks and whites continue in the USA. There are many people who think of themselves as Christians, but who inwardly harbor racist thoughts and feelings. Can a person be a Christian and refuse to part with inner racist thoughts? Can a person be a Christian if they refuse to behave in the way that the Bible defines Christian behavior? The Bible deals with this question in Hebrews 12.

> And have you forgotten the exhortation that addresses you as sons? "My son, do not regard lightly the discipline of the Lord, nor be weary when reproved by him. For the Lord disciplines the one he loves, and chastises every son whom he receives." It is for discipline that you have to endure. God is treating you as sons. For what son is there whom his father does not discipline? If you are left without discipline, in which all have participated, then you are illegitimate children and not sons. Besides this, we have had earthly fathers who disciplined us and we respected them. Shall we not much more be subject to the Father of spirits and live? For they disciplined us for a short time as it seemed best to

---

[14] Bryan Stevenson, *Just Mercy* (New York,: Spiegel & Grau, 2015 Paperback Edition). This is a powerful book, written by a black attorney who is a graduate of Harvard Law School. This book eloquently discusses some of the racism that Blacks have to contend with in the USA.

them, but he disciplines us for our good, that we may share his holiness.

Hebrews 12:5-10

This scripture makes it clear that one cannot simply say "I am going to be on the Lord's side, and I will do whatever I desire!" This is how King David behaved with Bathsheba! David proclaimed that he was following the Lord, but he took time out to engage in a sexual relationship with Bathsheba. Bathsheba was married to Uriah who fought in David's army. Bathsheba told David she was pregnant and then David compounded his sin of adultery by arranging to have Uriah in the front lines of the fighting. David wrote a letter to Joab and sent it by the hand of Uriah. In the letter he wrote, "Set Uriah in the forefront of the hardest fighting, and then draw back from him, that he may be struck down, and die" 2 Samuel 11:14. Uriah was killed in battle, according to David's instructions, and then David married Bathsheba. We read in 2 Samuel 11:27 "But the thing that David had done displeased the LORD."

David Confessed, But Paid A Steep Price

The Lord sent Nathan the prophet to David, and Nathan pronounced the Lord's judgment upon David for his sin.

> Thus says the LORD, the God of Israel, 'I anointed you king over Israel, and I delivered you out of the hand of Saul. And I gave you your master's house and your master's wives into your arms and gave you the house of Israel and of Judah. And if this were too little, I would add to you as much more. Why have you despised the word of the LORD, to do what is evil in his sight? You have struck down Uriah the Hittite with the sword and have taken his

wife to be your wife and have killed him with the sword of the Ammonites. Now therefore the sword shall never depart from your house, because you have despised me and have taken the wife of Uriah the Hittite to be your wife.' [11] Thus says the LORD, 'Behold, I will raise up evil against you out of your own house. And I will take your wives before your eyes and give them to your neighbor, and he shall lie with your wives in the sight of this sun. For you did it secretly, but I will do this thing before all Israel and before the sun.'" David said to Nathan, "I have sinned against the LORD." And Nathan said to David, "The LORD also has put away your sin; you shall not die. Nevertheless, because by this deed you have utterly scorned the LORD, the child who is born to you shall die."

2 Samuel 12:7-14

Nathan pronounced a severe judgment of God upon David, although he told David that God has put away his sin, because David did confess his sin to God (2 Samuel 12:13). God forgave David, but the judgment for his sin is that *the sword shall never depart from his house* ("I shall raise up evil against you out of your own house." 2 Samuel 12:11). This is in keeping with the Biblical principle that God disciplines his children (Psalm 94:12, Job 5:17).

My son, do not regard lightly the discipline of the Lord, nor be weary when reproved by him. For the Lord disciplines the one he loves, and chastises every son whom he receives."

Hebrews 12:5-6

The discipline David received was indeed severe. The child born of Bathsheba died (2 Samuel 12:15-18). This is a punishment that came to David as a direct result of his sin with Uriah and Bathsheba. This is clearly stated in 2 Samuel 12:10 ("Now therefore the sword shall never depart from your house, because you have despised me and have taken the wife of Uriah the Hittite to be your wife."). The Bible says that the punishment of "the sword" came upon David because of his sin with Uriah and Bathsheba ("Nevertheless, because by this deed you have utterly scorned the LORD, the child who is born to you shall die", 2 Samuel 12:14).

More was yet to come. Absalom, David's son, had a beautiful sister, Tamar. She was raped by David's son Ammon (2 Samuel 13:14). Absalom hated his brother Amman, because Ammon had violated his sister (2 Samuel 13:22). Absalom ordered his servants to kill Ammon, and they did (2 Samuel 13:28-29). Absalom plots against David to try and replace David as King. Absalom fails in this plot, and is killed by Joab (2 Samuel 18:14). When David hears of the death of his son Absalom, he is deeply grieved.

> And the king was deeply moved and went up to the chamber over the gate and wept. And as he went, he said, "O my son Absalom, my son, my son Absalom! Would I had died instead of you, O Absalom, my son, my son!"
>
> 2 Samuel 18:33

Thus we have traced the sad aftermath of David's sin with Bathsheba. *The consequences were catastrophic.* A baby son died. Another son of David, Ammon, raped David's daughter. A son of David, Absalom, murdered Ammon, a son of David. David's son Absalom tried to remove the crown from David's head and take it himself. David's son Absalom is killed by Joab. What a profusion of terrible consequences. And still, God forgave David, and considered David a man after God's own heart (1 Samuel 13:14, Acts 13:22).

Did David think that he would get away with his sin? Did David think that his affair with Bathsheba would receive no judgment from God? Adultery and murder had both been proscribed earlier in the laws of Moses and David would have been well aware of this. The reason that David's punishment was listed in great detail was precisely so that people would know that God "disciplines those whom he loves." Let David's punishment be a loud trumpet proclaiming that he who violates God's standards will suffer, as David did!!!

Is It Sin To Entertain Racist Thoughts?

Paul gave us a biblical definition of racism in Philippians 2:3 ("...in humility count others more significant than yourselves"). Someone replies to this by saying, I am not guilty of racism because I do not engage in racist actions, even though racist thoughts might be in my mind occasionally. But remember the teaching of Jesus in the Sermon on the Mount:

> You have heard that it was said, 'You shall not commit adultery.' But I say to you that everyone who looks at a woman with lustful intent has already committed adultery with her in his heart.
>
> Matthew 5:27-28

If one does not commit adultery by their actions, but looks at a woman with "lustful intent" then that person has already committed adultery in their heart. In the same manner we may say that if one person looks at another with "racist thoughts," then that is tantamount to "racist sins."

If your inner conviction is "white is better than black," or "white is better than brown", or "white is better than yellow," then you are guilty of the sin of racism. What are you to do with such thoughts? You are to repent. This includes confession. A prayer such as follows would be appropriate: Lord, I confess my sin of racism, and I ask for your forgiveness. And I ask you, Oh Holy Spirit to transform my thoughts so that they will conform to Paul's words in Philippians 2:3, "in humility count others more significant than yourselves."

Now just hold on a minute, I could perhaps count others as *equally* significant, but I will not count others as *more* significant. The clear teaching of Scripture is that we are to count others as <u>more significant than ourselves</u>. If I am not willing to do this then I can not say that I am endeavoring to be an obedient Christian. And if I hold on to my racist thoughts, then I am asking for God's judgment and discipline to come upon me, just as it came to David. *David paid a heavy price for his adultery with Bathsheba and so we will pay a heavy price for holding on to racist thoughts.* Better to repent and seek God's will.

Sadly, racism is still alive today in the USA. I saw the other day in the news a horrific example. An eighty-four-year-old Asian man was killed for no apparent reason on the streets of San Francisco. Police labeled this a "hate crime". The video shown by ABC is painful to watch, as it was a totally unprovoked daytime attack, and the eighty-four-year-old man had no opportunity even to defend himself. The attacker approached him from behind and violently knocked him to the ground. The eighty-four-year-old was killed in this attack.[15] This brings to mind the Scripture:

> deliver me from those who work evil, and save me from bloodthirsty men... Each evening they come back, howling like dogs and prowling about the city.
>
> Psalm 59:2, 59:6

Racist thoughts result in many violent actions. Those who commit racist sins will be punished for their sin.

---

[15] ABC 7 News, January 31, 2021.

You, Lᴏʀᴅ God of hosts, are God of Israel. Rouse
yourself to punish all the nations; spare none of
those who treacherously plot evil.

Psalm 59:5

This is one of the great comforts of being a Christian and
believing Christian teaching. We know that sin will be judged,
transgression will be punished, justice will prevail. The racist *will*
be punished for their willful racism!! So my racist brothers and
sisters, what will you do with those inner thoughts and inclinations
that white is better than yellow and black and brown!! Flee these
thoughts, with God's help. Repent, confess your sins before God.
Pray, *Lord deliver me from racism.*

The Biblical teaching is that God will discipline his children
when they disobey God's will. David paid a severe price for his
disobedience. And so will any child of God who presumes upon
God's grace. The Bible is crystal clear in teaching that racism is
contrary to God's will. And a white person, or any other person who
practices racism will be disciplined for their sin by the judgment of
God, just as David was punished by God. Any white believer who
thinks that a black person, or a darker skinned person is inferior in
any way because of the color of their skin is guilty of serious sin,
and needs to pray, "Lord, forgive me for my sin of racism and by the
power of your Holy Spirit change me, so that I will love my neighbor
as myself."

It Is Time For The Church To Say Racism Is Sinful!

The Christian Church must speak up for racial equality!!! *It is time
for the church to proclaim loudly and clearly that racism is contrary to
Biblical teaching.* Racist acts will not go unpunished by God.

> Now may our God and Father himself, and our Lord Jesus direct our way to you, and may the Lord make you increase and abound in love for one another and for all, as we do for you, so that he may establish your hearts blameless in holiness before our God and Father, at the coming of our Lord Jesus with all his saints
>
> 1 Thessalonians 2:11-13

Abound in loving each other more and more. There is no room for racism here. How can one consider another race lesser, if he is to love all races more and more?

The two most important commands in the Bible are 1) Love God with all your heart, and 2) love your neighbor as yourself. We can conclude therefore that the two biggest sins in the Bible are to violate the two greatest commandments. So the two greatest sins are: 1) Not loving God, and 2) not loving your neighbor.

Violating the second greatest commandment is to go against "Love your neighbor as yourself." One of the most concise statements of violating the second greatest commandment is found in Philippians 2:

> Do nothing from selfish ambition or conceit, but in humility count others more significant than yourselves. Let each of you look not only to his own interests, but also to the interests of others. Have this mind among yourselves, which is yours in Christ Jesus, who, though he was in the form of God, did not count equality with God a thing to be grasped, but emptied himself, by taking the form of a servant, being born in the likeness of men. And being found in human form, he humbled himself

by becoming obedient to the point of death, even
death on a cross.

Philippians 2:3-8

The phrase "in humility count others more significant than
yourselves" is a *nuclear bomb exploding in the midst of racism*! If we
follow the Biblical exhortation "count others more significant than
yourselves," a permanent death blow is struck to racism of any kind!
For what is racism but to think of myself as better in some manner
than someone else on account of my race. The Ku Klux Klansman
thinks of himself as superior to the man with dark skin, the Higher
caste person in India thinks of himself as superior to the darker
skinned person. The lighter skinned people in Latin America think
of themselves as superior to the darker skinned people in Latin
America. The Aryan German considered himself superior to the
Jew. These are examples of racism. The Bible says racism is a sin.

If you have been motivated by racist thoughts, it will take a
miracle of God's power to free you. It will take a miracle of God's
power to help you love your neighbor as yourself. How can you pray
the Lord's prayer and at the same time harbor racist feelings? When
you pray, "Lord, may your will be done," also pray "Lord, please free
me from racist thoughts and feelings, so that I may truly love my
neighbor, and so that I may seek your will in my relationships with
all other races."

...but in humility count others more significant
than yourselves.

Philippians 2:3

CHAPTER 8
Looking to Jesus

Let us run with endurance the race that is set before
us, looking to Jesus, the founder and perfecter of
our faith,

Hebrews 12:1

One of the most amazing chapters ever written on the subject
of faith is Hebrews 11. In this chapter we have the powerful
results that are accomplished by faith. Some giants of faith in the
Old Testament are listed, including Abraham, Sarah, Isaac, Jacob,
Joseph, and Moses (Hebrews 11:17-25)

The faith of ordinary men and women accomplished amazing
feats which are recorded for all time in Hebrews chapter eleven.
It would not be far off the mark to say that Chapter 11 Hebrews
contains a condensed version of some of the mightiest acts in history!
All these awesome deeds were accomplished through the faith of
ordinary men and women.

Faith Grows By Looking To Jesus

After reading Hebrews 11 we are left with a deep yearning for the kind of faith that was exhibited by the saints in Hebrews 11.

If faith is this powerful, if faith is necessary in order to please God ("without faith it is impossible to please him, for whoever would draw near to God must believe that he exists and that he rewards those who seek him" Hebrews 11:6), if faith can accomplish such mighty acts, then it would seem that Hebrews 11 was written with one main objective in mind. That objective is to engender in the reader a strong desire to have this kind of strong faith!!

Upon finishing reading Hebrews chapter eleven our prayer might be: Lord, please show me what I can do to have a faith like this. One would hope that soon after finishing Hebrews 11 there would be given to us the answer to this prayer. And Lo and Behold, here it is! As soon as we start the next chapter, we find the answer!

> ...let us run with endurance the race that is set before us, looking to Jesus, the founder and perfecter of our faith, who for the joy that was set before him endured the cross, despising the shame, and is seated at the right hand of the throne of God.
>
> Hebrews 12:1-2

"Looking to Jesus," will help our faith to grow like the giants of faith that we read about in Hebrews 11. Here are two riveting comments on how we are to engage in "looking to Jesus." John the Baptist, at the beginning of his ministry, introduced Jesus to the first disciples. John the Baptist knew much about Jesus, and could have mentioned any one of various characteristics of Jesus. It is very significant that John chose the following introduction:

> The next day he saw Jesus coming toward him, and said, "Behold, the Lamb of God, who takes away the sin of the world!"
>
> John 1:29

He proclaimed Jesus as the one who had come into the world as the great sacrifice for sin. This helps us understand what it means to "look at Jesus." The main thought we are to have about Jesus as we look to him is that his death on the cross brought about the forgiveness of our sins. This is confirmed by Paul's words in 1 Corinthians 15:3, where he said that the most important teaching in the Bible is that *Christ died for our sins.* So the most significant thing we can do when we "look to Jesus" is to pray "thank you Lord, for taking my sins upon yourself on the cross so that my sins may be forgiven." This is the first and most God-pleasing action we can take as we "run with endurance the race that is set before us."

In Revelation 14:1, John the disciple spoke of what he saw in his vision looking inside the pearly gates. Notice that he does not say that he saw streets of gold, or a river flowing down the central thoroughfare. The first thing his eyes landed upon was:

> Then I looked, and behold, on Mount Zion stood the Lamb."
>
> Revelation 14:1

John is saying that the most important point about heaven is *"the lamb of God."* The Lamb is the one who takes away the sin of the world. The main attraction of heaven is the Lamb.

"Looking to Jesus" does not mean look at him only when we go to church, or only while we are engaged in prayer, or only while we are facing some serious trial, although these are certainly most appropriate times to be "looking to Jesus." It means we are to look to Jesus while we are engaged in the "race that is before us," the entirety of the Christian life. So, look to Jesus continually!!

As we look to Jesus, how are we to look at him? What shall we think of him? What aspect of him shall be held in our minds? There are several aspects of Christ that we could reflect upon, such as his words while he defended the rights of the oppressed or the miracles he performed to alleviate our suffering. No. It is none of these. What is the most important aspect of Jesus Christ? John the Baptist announced it when he said "The Lamb of God who takes away the sins of the world." So when we look to Jesus let us meditate upon the most important thing that Jesus did: he died on the cross for our sins.

> In him we have redemption through his blood, the
> forgiveness of our trespasses, according to the riches
> of his grace, which he lavished upon us,
>
> Ephesians 1:7-8

The Riches Of Christ Are Inexhaustible

Paul the Apostle says the riches of Christ are unsearchable. The more you take of the riches of Christ, the more there is. How does one explain this? The more you take of the riches of Christ, the greater will be your understanding of what he has done for you on the Cross. So, the more you take, the more there is!

When we have sung Christ's praises with all the talents of a Mozart or a Bach, surely we will have praised him enough, and we can rest. No, that is not the case. Remember the final stanza of Newton's wonderful Amazing Grace, "When we've been there ten thousand years, bright shining as the sun, we've no less days to sing God's praise than when we'd first begun."

The Psalm writer said "I will praise you more and more (Psalm 71:14)."

Many of these riches will come to you in the future. Does this mean that he will do more in the future than he has in the past? NO.

He has already done all that he needs to do for 1 Corinthians 15:3 to be the most important teaching in the Bible. Yes, he will do more for us in the future. For every time he interacts with us he behaves toward us with steadfast love and he is acting in a gracious manner toward us, but as far as what he does that makes 1 Corinthians 15:3 the most important teaching in the Bible, he has done that already. He did it once, and does not need to do it again.

The concept of the Lamb of God taking the sins of the world upon himself is an idea which could have originated only from God. Can you imagine a representative from humans (such as Moses) going to God and saying "Lord, would you please die for all our sins so that we would not have to die for them?" I doubt that even the most inventive and assertive of all the angels would ever have come up with the idea of God giving his only son to die for us on the cross. And when God announced in heaven that this was his plan I suspect that the angels were astonished! Such a majestic strategy could only have originated in the heart and mind of God.

> And we all, with unveiled face, beholding the glory
> of the Lord are being transformed into the same
> image from one degree of glory to another. For this
> comes from the Lord who is the Spirit.
>
> 2 Corinthians 3:18

As we "look to Jesus and his glory" the Holy Spirit is at work transforming us into his image, from glory to glory. Is this not one of the greatest supernatural works that can occur within us while we are upon this earth? So look unto Jesus, and be transformed!

Some of you may be thinking you need to be better before you can look to him. No. Come and look as you are. Come now. For you are already clothed in royal garments. Look unto the Lord at this moment, no matter your condition or your feelings. We can come to him at any time because we are clothed in his robe of righteousness.

I will greatly rejoice in the LORD; my soul shall exult in my God, for he has clothed me with the garments of salvation he has covered me with the robe of righteousness,

Isaiah 61:10

Whenever you look at him, may his countenance remind you that you are dressed in his righteousness. If you are one of the people who always think of their own sin and frailty, remember that you are clothed with his righteousness. Here is another great paradox of the Bible: in my own clothes, a sinner; but in Christ, righteous!!!

There is therefore now no condemnation for those who are in Christ Jesus.

Romans 8:1

God Desires That We See His Glory

The stars in the sky are meant to be seen by us. Why else would they be there, shining so splendiferously every night? They are like the promises in Scripture, meant for us to look at them. There are countless stars above, shining brilliantly, each one different, each one with great power. The promises of God in the Bible are similar to the stars in this respect. They are great and powerful, waiting only for us to look at them! At times we refuse to look. Instead we stare at the speed bump in the road and gaze at the garbage heaps. Lift your eyes, and look upon the stars. Look at the promises of God, all of them, any one of which has great power to lift and inspire. Look at all of them, and be lifted up!

By which he has granted to us his precious and very great promises, so that through them you may become partakers of the divine nature, having escaped from the corruption that is in the world because of sinful desire.

2 Peter 1:4

There is one who is more brilliant than all the stars. And that one is Jesus Christ. Look at him now and be dazzled! It is not possible for him to fail to dazzle you when you look unto him in faith. We may think that there is a similarity between Jesus Christ and the sun because the sun is the brightest object in the heavens. But the sun only seems to be the brightest because it is far closer to us than the other stars. But Jesus is the brightest not because he is the closest to us but because he is *inherently* of his own self, brighter than all the stars in the heavens.

The lesser praises the greater, The stars are commanded to praise the Lord. All the combined brightness of the stars does not approach the brilliance of our Lord Jesus.

> Praise him, sun and moon, praise him, all you shining stars!

Psalms 148:3

Next time you look up to the sky, yes, enjoy the brightness of the countless lights above, but always remember that there is one whose brightness far exceeds the combined luminosity of all the countless stars, and that is Jesus Christ. Gaze upon him, and enjoy his brilliance! Gaze upon him. Lord Jesus, I look to you now, to overcome all the darkness of the enemy, and to lead me in triumph always, forever and ever!

What if you make an effort to look at the Lord and he is not there? What if I turn my head too slowly to catch him, and he had time to move away? Is it possible for me to choose to look to Jesus, and find that he is not there? No! Remember the promise in Matthew 28:20, And behold, I am with you always, to the end of the age.

Jesus has promised that he is always with us to the end of the age. So no matter at what moment in time I choose to look to the Lord, he is there. Now Always. To the end of the age. By my side. This presence of his in a location where I can always see him is not something that I deserve or earn or work my way up to my by my godly behavior. It is a gift. By grace.

God desires for me to see him more clearly than I do presently. Well, then why is it such a struggle? Why does it seem like I can grunt and groan and flex all my muscles in the pursuit of knowing him more intimately without receiving a greater reward? Jesus prayed for us,

> Father, I desire that they also, whom you have given me, may be with me where I am, to see my glory that you have given me because you loved me before the foundation of the world.
>
> John 17:24

It is an amazing indication of Christ's love for us that *he desires* for us to see his glory. Jesus desire this for his children. Seeing his glory is something far more magnificent than anything we can imagine. Paul had some personal experiences like this.

> I will go on to visions and revelations of the Lord. I know a man in Christ who fourteen years ago was caught up to the third heaven—whether in the body or out of the body I do not know, God knows. And I know that this man was caught up into paradise—whether in the body or out of the body I do not know, God knows
>
> 2 Corinthians 12:1-3

> What no eye has seen, nor ear heard, nor the heart of man imagined, what God has prepared for those who love him"
>
> 1 Corinthians 2:9

To see the glory of Christ comes from a supernatural enablement. It is not something we can bring about by our own wisdom or strength. It is something that is beyond what our heart can imagine or our mind can conceive. It can come only by the aid of the Holy Spirit, as stated in John's Gospel.

> When the Spirit of truth comes, he will guide you into all the truth, for he will not speak on his own authority, but whatever he hears he will speak, and he will declare to you the things that are to come. He will glorify me, for he will take what is mine and declare it to you. All that the Father has is mine; therefore I said that he will take what is mine and declare it to you.
>
> John 16:13-16

Holy Spirit, you have said you will guide me into all truth, and that you will guide me to see the glory of Christ. I pray to you now, Oh Holy Spirit, help me to see Christ more clearly. Help me to see the glory of Christ.

Looking At Jesus Overcomes Demonic Power

Another great example of faith was shown by a Canaanite Woman whose daughter was possessed by a demon. She came to Jesus and asked for a healing.

At first he did not answer her. She persisted, and he replied "woman, great is your faith! Be it done for you as you desire. And her daughter was healed instantly (Matthew 15:28)." Jesus was pleased by the great faith of the woman. Faith in Jesus Christ can expel a demon.

I had an experience with this around the seventh year of serving as a Pastor.

I was in my office one afternoon counseling with a member. My secretary interrupted and said you have an emergency phone call. I took the call, and it was an engineer I knew. I knew him and his wife from several previous encounters. He was extremely level headed, and very analytical, like most engineers. He said Walter, I am at home, please come over immediately. The note of desperation in his voice was compelling. I said I will be there in five minutes. I told the person I was talking to that I had an emergency, and we would reschedule. I started driving toward the home of my engineer friend. I got to within about two blocks of his home, and I remember a dark and foreboding feeling. I knocked on the door. The man came to the door, pointed me to the living room, and left for other parts of the house. In the living room was his wife. I knew her. I had met her several times, but this time there was something different. She looked familiar, but there was a snarl and a strange countenance. She spoke to me. I knew her voice, but she spoke with a voice that was different from the voice I had heard her speak with before. It was a dark voice, a malevolent voice. The voice was coming out of her mouth, and her lips were moving in accord with the words she was speaking, but it was if someone else was speaking thru her.

I will never forget her first words to me. "What are you doing here holy man? You will not get me out of here."

I remember my total surprise and shock. Nobody had ever addressed me that way. *You will not get me out of here, Holy Man.* I did not want to believe what I started to think might be happening. I had never experienced anything like this before in my whole life, although I had read about such things in the Gospels. What do I do now? I felt like turning around and going home. But the husband was clearly terrified, and had no idea how to cope with this situation.

I stayed. But I was afraid. There was a feeling of evil in the room that was frightening and dark. Far worse and more real than the most frightening movie I had ever seen.

The voice said, "you can't get me out of here. I am strong. I can make that phone ring." Within seconds the phone rang. *I was not about to answer it.* Now, I was really scared.

Then she, or the voice, said to me, "you see that table over there," and she pointed to the dining room table. I can make that table move. Do you want to see me make that table move?" It was said as a dare, a challenge, in fact a sneer. I thought about what to say. I didn't want to say yes…because I thought, if I said yes, I knew, without a doubt, what would happen. That table would move. It was absolutely clear that there was a power in that room far greater than any power or strength that I possessed. Also, I did not want to say "yes", because I felt somehow that the voice wanted me to say yes.

Do you want to see me make that table move? It was daring me to say yes. It wanted me to say yes. And if I said yes, I thought I would be yielding in some way, or agreeing with, this power. So I did not say "yes". I thought about saying NO. If I said NO, I would be acknowledging that this power *was able* to move that table if it chose to, and I would again be yielding in some way to this greater power. So I did not say NO. That did not leave me with much to say.

It was clear to me that this woman was behaving as if she was possessed by a demon. There were many such instances in the Gospels. I don't know whether at that time I believed that she was possessed by a demon or not, but she was clearly behaving as if she was. So I decided I would treat her that way. I would treat her as if she was possessed by a demon. I had read the Gospels enough that I knew what to do. I started quoting Scripture. In particular I read Colossians 2:13-15,

"And you, who were dead in trespasses and the uncircumcision of your flesh, God made alive together with him, having forgiven us all our trespasses, having canceled the bond which stood against us with its legal demands; this he set aside, nailing it to the cross. He disarmed the principalities and powers and made a public example of them, triumphing over them in him."

The moment I read from the Bible, she screamed, shrieked, and tried to hit me. She said again, "you won't get me out of here." Same evil, malevolent feeling in the room.

I was about to give up, thinking, *Well maybe I don't know how to do one of these demon exorcisms. Maybe the Bible isn't working. Maybe it won't do any good to keep reading the Bible.*

Then it was as if a quiet inner voice whispered to me, and urged me on. *Go ahead Walter, you are doing the right thing.*

And I thought, Jesus IS stronger than the devil. Greater is he that is in us, than he that is in the world. The devil *must* respond to the power of Jesus Christ. This demon WILL respond to the power of Jesus Christ. And I read out loud from the Bible again, commanding the demon to obey the Word of God: "Having canceled the bond which stood against us,,,this he set aside, nailing it to the cross. He disarmed the principalities and powers, triumphing over them in him."

I said, "demon, devil, come out of her, because Jesus has defeated you on the Cross.... he has defeated you... Leave!!!" There was a sigh.

She looked up at me, and before she said anything, I knew this was the person I had known before. This was her normal face and she said "Walter, what are you doing here?"

The whole atmosphere of the room changed. Back to normal. The demon was gone.

Why do I tell you about this? Because I want us to know that evil does exist. There is such a thing. The Bible is correct in what it says about the devil and evil. Otherwise why would Jesus have ever said "Deliver us from evil?" Another thing I learned from this experience: the power of the devil and demons is far greater than our own power. When I was in that room, and the woman said "do you want me to move that table?" I sensed in a deep way, that no power on earth could have stood against the power in that room.

We could get the offensive line of the Seattle Seahawks, five guys, 300 lbs each…side by side…they could all get together and hold on to the table. It still would have moved. The devil laughs at our efforts. That is why Jesus taught us to pray Father, deliver us from evil… because we do not have the strength in our own to fight evil.

There is only one power that has an effect on the devil and his demons: and that is the power of Jesus Christ. Martin Luther knew the reality of the devil. That is why he wrote the words in the third stanza of the Hymn "A Mighty Fortress": "The prince of darkness grim, we tremble not for him, his rage we can endure for lo his doom is sure. One little word shall fell him." One little word shall fell him. The word that will fell him, that will defeat the devil, is the word Jesus Christ. The most wonderful and powerful word in the English language. When we speak in the name of Jesus Christ, we speak with God's authority, and the devil trembles.

As Christians we do not need to live in terror of the devil and evil. Because the Bible says "Greater is he that is in us, than he that is in the world! 1 John 4:4." Yes I do believe that there is such a thing as demon possession. Witchcraft and devil worship are real, and the Bible says we are to stay away from them.

This business of resisting evil is a tricky business, because many acts which the Bible says are sin, are sanctioned by our culture. Materialism, sexual relations outside of marriage, pornography, violence in movies and TV, other addictions. These are, to a large degree, condoned by our society. We are surrounded by them. We do not, in and of ourselves, have the strength to resist these evils. Will you ask God now to help deliver you from evil? Father, deliver us from evil.

CS Lewis wrote that the greatest accomplishment of the devil is to convince people that he does not exist!!! For Christians, the conclusive evidence lies with the words and actions of Jesus. Jesus said in John 8:44 to those who did not believe in him: "You belong to your father, the devil, and you want to carry out your father's desire. He was a murderer from the beginning,.. for he is a liar and the father of lies."

During the forty days in the wilderness temptation, Jesus spoke to the devil. Clearly Jesus believed in the existence of the devil. Jesus said that there IS evil, there is a devil. That settles the question. I know there are Christians who do not believe there is a devil. They say, well, it was the times in which Jesus lived. Jesus was simply following the views of the age in which he lives. But the times in which Jesus lived did not teach what Jesus taught. Jesus taught that evil was so real, and so far removed from God, that we need redemption by God himself. This was not a prevalent idea at all in the times of Jesus. Jesus was teaching something radically new and different!!

Some people say there is a devil, but it doesn't make logical sense to say there is a devil. Remember, we did not come to Jesus Christ through our logic, but by the revealed word of God. We did not learn about the cross and forgiveness of our sins through our logic, but by revelation from the Bible. The deepest secrets of Christianity were not uncovered by our logical minds penetrating layers of complex thought. So we do not learn about the devil by our logical mind, but by revelation from the word of God. Jesus has said, there IS a devil. That settles it!

When Facing My Black Dogs

I have mentioned that I often struggle with my emotions. They go up, and down. Churchill called his depressions his black dogs. I resonate with his term *"my black dogs."* The other day I was experiencing one of my black dogs. I thought about the words "looking to Jesus," so I started looking to Jesus on the Cross. It came to me that while he was on the cross he experienced separation from God, which caused him to suffer intensely, and yet his response was to trust in God, and address him as "My God." I thought about my response to my black dogs, and I thought about my response at this very moment. I was not responding the way that Jesus responded. This realization helped me to move toward the attitude described in Psalm 71:14 "I will praise you yet more and more." And as I praised him more and more, the black dogs lost some of their power to sneer and growl!

There are many passages in the Old Testament where we are urged to "look to the Lord."

> But my eyes are toward you, O GOD, my Lord; in you I seek refuge; leave me not defenseless!
>
> Psalm 141.8

> My eyes are ever toward the LORD, for he will pluck my feet out of the net. Turn to me and be gracious to me, for I am lonely and afflicted.
>
> Psalm 25:15

> To you I lift up my eyes, O you who are enthroned in the heavens! Behold, as the eyes of servants look to the hand of their master, as the eyes of a maidservant to the hand of her mistress, so our

eyes look to the LORD our God, till he has mercy upon us.

Psalm 123:1-2

For we are powerless against this great horde that is coming against us. We do not know what to do, but our eyes are on you"…Do not be afraid and do not be dismayed at this great horde, for the battle is not yours but God's.

2 Chronicles 20:12

I have set the LORD always before me; because he is at my right hand, I shall not be shaken. Therefore my heart is glad, and my whole being rejoices; my flesh also dwells secure.

Psalm 16:8

By studying the above Scriptures we see that *"looking to the Lord"* elicits a great amount of assistance from God in all kinds of perilous situations. It is to my benefit to look to the Lord with great frequency.

The Los Angeles Marathon is a big annual event in the Los Angeles area!! Thousands of people watch this race, either in person, or on television. What a strange sight it would be if all the runners were straining their necks, turning them around, so that they would be looking *behind* at the most recent one hundred yards that that they have just run. Necks would become sore and strained from looking behind. Many runners would bump into strange objects, and their progress would be hindered by continually looking back rather than looking forward. It would be a strange sight, would it not? An experienced runner would advise the runners to look forward rather than backwards. This is the advice that the writer of Hebrews gives to his fellow runners:

...let us run with endurance the race that is set before us, looking to Jesus, the founder and perfecter of our faith, who for the joy that was set before him endured the cross, despising the shame, and is seated at the right hand of the throne of God.

Hebrews 12:1-2

Remember the phrase "looking to Jesus" is given immediately following Hebrews 11, the great chapter on faith. Looking to Jesus is one of the methods given to us of how to strengthen our faith, and keep it growing. Looking at Jesus does not mean a passing glance, as when looking at a roadside billboard. It means a long searching look, while thinking about the most important teaching in the Bible.

Permit me to give you an exercise now which will bless you. Sit in a chair, close your eyes, and look to Jesus for five minutes. Look at him with hope, adoration, love and worship.

As you look at him, thank him and praise him that he is the Lamb of God who took away your sins. As you look, something supernatural will happen. Any one, or all, of the items mentioned in 2 Corinthians 3:18 ("And we all, with unveiled face, beholding the glory of the Lord are being transformed into the same image from one degree of glory to another") will take place. What a profitable use of five minutes.

Try it now.

CHAPTER 9
The Sovereignty of God

Whatever the Lord pleases, He does.

Psalm 135:6

There are no accidents in our lives, no mistakes, and nothing can occur which ought not to occur. If I have in abundance, he gave it to me. If I should lose all I have, it is better that I should lose than have. "We know that all things work together for good to them that love God (Romans 8:28)."

Scriptures That Speak Of God's Sovereignty

Is God actually able to work all things together for good, and to bring about always what is best for me? Yes, because God is sovereign. Here are some of the Biblical passages which set forth God's sovereignty.

I blessed the Most High, and praised and honored him who lives forever, for his dominion is an everlasting dominion, and his kingdom endures from generation to generation; all the inhabitants of the earth are accounted as nothing, and he does according to his will among the host of heaven and among the inhabitants of the earth; and none can stay his hand or say to him, "What have you done?"

Daniel 4:34-35

God reigns over the nations; God sits on his holy throne. The princes of the peoples gather as the people of the God of Abraham. For the shields of the earth belong to God; he is highly exalted!

Psalm 17:8-9

Our God is in the heavens; he does all that he pleases.

Psalm 115:3

Whatever the LORD pleases, he does, In heaven and on earth, in the seas and all deeps.

Psalm 135:6

How beautiful upon the mountains are the feet of him who brings good news, who publishes peace, who brings good news of happiness, who publishes salvation, who says to Zion, "Your God reigns.

Isaiah 52.7

Then I heard what seemed to be the voice of a great multitude, like the roar of many waters and like the sound of mighty peals of thunder, crying out, "Hallelujah! For the Lord our God the Almighty reigns.

Revelation 19:6

The sovereignty of God is the biblical doctrine which states that God reigns and he is in control of everything in our universe. He has power over everything, and does whatever he chooses to do. Nothing catches him by surprise.

If God reigns and does whatever he pleases, then whatever he does is pleasing to him. If God is pleased, then can I be pleased?

A Stanford Physics Professor And The Existence Of Paradoxes In The Bible.

In studying the Bible, we find a great number of paradoxes. A *paradox* is defined as a statement that, despite logical reasoning from acceptable premises, leads to a conclusion that seems logically unacceptable, or self-contradictory. Many people struggle with the paradoxes in the Bible. It presents a challenge for many people who do not know precisely how to treat paradoxes in the Bible. They understand paradoxes as evidence that at least one of the poles of a dual paradox must be false.

For instance, Leonard Susskind, a Professor of Physics at Stanford, says:

> Scientists – real scientists- resist the temptation to explain natural phenomena, including creation itself, by divine intervention... So we resist, to

the death, all explanations of the world based on anything but the laws of physics, mathematics, and probability.[16]

Susskind believes that creation by divine intervention is unacceptable (resist it to the death!) because this would require a violation of the laws of physics, mathematics and probability.

It is highly ironic that Susskind's statement about "resisting to the death all explanations of the world based on anything but the laws of physics, mathematics and probability" is based on the presupposition that all the "laws of science" behave in a logical and consistent manner. I say ironic because Richard Feynman believes that all the "laws of physics" do *not* behave in a logical and consistent manner. Richard Feynman (generally considered one of the greatest Physicists of the 20th century) said:

> [Quantum mechanics] describes nature as absurd from the point of view of common sense. And yet it fully agrees with experiment. So I hope you can accept nature as She is - absurd.[17]

Feynman is saying that the laws of quantum mechanics describing nature are not logical, because nature itself does not always behave according to common sense, or logic. So we cannot say that the laws of nature support the view that nothing supernatural can occur. I mention this here because it is not logically consistent to say that a paradox in the Bible is logically inconsistent with reality, since the laws that govern reality itself (nature), according to Feynman, are not always logically self-consistent (as in quantum mechanics).

---

[16] Leonard Susskind, *The Cosmic Landscape* (New York,: Back Bay Books, 2006), 355.
[17] Richard Feynman, QED, *The Strange Theory of Light and Matter* (Princeton University Press, Princeton, New Jersey, 1985), p. 10

The main point here is that science and nature do contain paradoxes. So we need not conclude that paradoxes are problematic and opposed to scientific thinking if they exist in the Bible.

If God Is Sovereign And Good, Why Is There Evil and Suffering?

Many believe that the most difficult question facing Christianity is the question of *theodicy*, which is: how can a good, loving God who is omnipotent allow human suffering and evil?

This is the problem that drove C.S. Lewis to agnosticism during the first part of his life. Speaking about our universe, Lewis wrote:

> All stories will come to nothing: all life will turn out in the end to have been a transitory and senseless contortion on the idiotic face of infinite matter. If you ask me to believe that this is the work of a benevolent and omnipresent spirit, I reply all the evidence points in the opposite direction. Either there is no spirit behind the universe, or else a spirit indifferent to good and evil, or else an evil spirit.[18]

> If God were good, he would wish to make his creatures perfectly happy, and if God were almighty He would be able to do what he wished. But the creatures are not happy. Therefore God lacks either goodness or power, or both. This is the problem of pain, in its simplest form.[19]

---

[18] Lewis, C.S., *The Problem of Pain*, (Harper, San Francisco, 2001), p. 3
[19] Op. Cit. p.16

Armand Nicholi, for 30 years a Professor of Psychiatry at Harvard, has written an excellent book which discusses the views of Freud and CS Lewis on the question of theodicy. Dr. Nicholi says:

> For Freud and for Lewis before his transition, the problem of reconciling the notion of an all-loving, benevolent Creator with human suffering presented the greatest obstacle to acceptance of the spiritual world-view. Indeed, the problem of pain and the related problem of evil have been central conundra for believers throughout history.
>
> Both Freud and Lewis asked, "If God is sovereign, if He really is in charge of the universe and if He really loves me, then how could he allow me to suffer so? Either He does not exist or He is not in control or He doesn't really care." Freud concluded He does not exist. Lewis concluded differently.[20]

After Lewis resolved this paradox for himself he argues at great length in "The Problem of Pain" that one cannot conclude that the framing of the problem of theodicy shows that the two aspects of the problem of theodicy cannot both be true. Lewis's book "The Problem of Pain," is the deepest study of this issue that I am familiar with, and I urge you to read Lewis's book.

Many great thinkers have held on to the paradox within the problem of theodicy to buttress their continued adherence to agnosticism, such as Freud. Lewis and Freud, early in their lives were pushed toward agnosticism by the problem of theodicy but each then took a different route. Lewis moved past the paradox and came to a

---

[20] Armand Nicholi, *The Question of God: CS Lewis and Sigmund Freud Debate God* (Free Press, New York 2002) pp. 187-188

strong faith in God, while Freud never did move past it to arrive at a faith in God and for most of his life was proud of being an atheist.

CS Lewis writes persuasively in his book "The Problem of Pain" that the paradox in the problem of theodicy does not logically forbid us from believing that there is an omnipotent and loving God. Lewis devotes the entire book to the subject of how to reconcile the love and omnipotence of God with the suffering in our world. Lewis says:

> The problem of reconciling human suffering with the existence of a God who loves, is only insoluble so long as we attach a trivial meaning to the word 'love.'[21]

When it comes to the attempt to reconcile the goodness of an omnipotent God with the existence of pain and suffering, it seems to me that this is one of the major paradoxes in the Bible, and the best we can do is to accept both sides of the paradox without the ability to reconcile by human logic the two sides of this paradox. Resolving this paradox may lie beyond our human ability to use our understanding and ability to reason. One solution is to conclude that at least one or both sides of the paradox must be false.

Some have opted to solve the paradox of theodicy by asking why God could not have created humans with free will, and at the same time made them in such a way that they would always chose the good. Then there would be no evil. Lewis says:

> If you choose to say 'God can give a creature free will and at the same time withhold free will from it', you have not succeeded in saying anything about God: meaningless combinations of words do not suddenly acquire meaning simply because we prefix to them the two other words 'God can'.

---

[21] Lewis, CS, *The Problem of Pain*, p.40

> It remains true that all things are possible with God: the intrinsic impossibilities are not things but nonentities. It is no more possible for God than for the weakest of His creatures to carry out both of two mutually exclusive alternatives; not because His power meets an obstacle, but because nonsense remains nonsense even when we talk it about God.[22]

By his own incarnation Jesus sheds light upon the mystery of good and suffering. Look at the life of Christ. He was pure goodness, but he suffered greatly. How can that be just? Jesus even asked from the cross, why ("My God, my God, why have you forsaken me?, Matthew 27:46). In my opinion, the final answer we can give remains a mystery. The life of Christ himself shows us that there can be great good and omnipotence in the midst of great suffering, without a fully logical reason that can answer how or why?

Jesus personifies by his own incarnation the ultimate union between good, evil and suffering. Evil was perpetrated upon Jesus when he suffered on the cross, and yet Jesus embodied goodness and never committed any evil deed. The question of God's goodness and suffering in the incarnation of Christ remains a mystery to the believer in Christ.

The sovereignty of God means that he is in control, whether I can fully understand him or not. What about the question asked when we began the discussion of theodicy at the beginning of this section. Did we fully answer the question? I would say no, we did not. My own answer to the paradox in theodicy is that I believe in both poles of the paradox: there is suffering, and God *is* absolutely good and omnipotent. And so the ultimate answer remains a mystery. Spurgeon's answer to the problem of theodicy well states the mystery involved. Spurgeon says:

---

[22] Op.cit. p. 18

the miracle of divine glory lies in this—that he has made men free agents, has endowed them with a will...and yet, such is the magnificent strategy of heaven, such is the marvellous force of the divine mind, that despite everything, the will of God is done... Can you understand it, for I cannot, how man is a free agent, a responsible agent, so that his sin is his own wilful sin and lies with him and never with God, and yet at the same time God's purposes are fulfilled. I cannot comprehend it: without hesitation I believe it, and rejoice so to do, I never hope to comprehend it. I worship a God I never expect to comprehend.[23]

God Says To Job, If You Know So Much, Tell Me What Is Inside An Electron.

During the course of his discussion with his three friends, Job accuses God of being unfair. (Job 19:5-11).

Then the Lord challenges Job,

> Where were you when I laid the foundation of the earth? Tell me, if you have understanding. Who determined its measurement - surely you know!
>
> Job 38:4-5

A modern day commentary of the above passages might read like this. The Lord questions Job: where were you when I launched the Big Bang? Can you explain where the first electron came from? Can you tell me the dimensions of an electron (although according

---

[23] Charles Spurgeon, The Metropolitan Tabernacle Pulpit, Volume 16 (Texas, Pilgrim Publications) p. 501

to quantum mechanics, we cannot ever know the actual dimensions of an electron...for it is never in one place! It might be here, it might be there). And furthermore, an electron might be a particle, or a wave, or neither. What is it?

Can you tell me what is inside an electron? Can you tell me about an "inflaton,"[24] since scientists say it was particles called inflatons that caused the initial inflation of the universe, a necessary part of the initial expansion of our universe, and a part of "The Big Bang Theory." And since we are on this subject, can you tell me whether the universe will continue to accelerate in its expansion, or will it begin to decelerate at some point. And what about *consciousness*, which some scientists believe is the greatest scientific mystery of all. Who has put self-awareness and understanding into the mind, and precisely where is it in the brain?

Who determined that a certain number would be the speed limit for all matter, so that matter is never able to travel faster than that number that is the speed of light? Science can measure what that number is, but is unable to explain why the speed of light is one particular number rather than some other number.

The above are all questions that scientists presently are not able to answer, although they probably will find answers to some of these questions in the future. God presently knows what is inside an electron, and he knows why the speed of light is the particular number that it is. God knows the answers to all the questions stated above, since God is sovereign and omniscient.

In no way is this intended as any kind of a criticism of science. Scientists have made tremendous progress and it is a tribute to science that we understand enough to even ask questions like the ones put forth here. God does know the precise answer to each of the questions set forth here. It is a tribute to the majestic sovereignty

---

[24] Alan Guth, *The Inflationary Universe*, (New York, Basic Books, a member of the Perseus Books Group) 1997, 233, 238-239. Guth is presently a Professor of Physics at MIT.

of God that he knows the answer to all the above questions, and to questions which we have not even imagined yet!

One of the lessons of Job is that when Job ceases to question God, and admits that God is sovereign, then Job receives an unexpected blessing. At the end of the book of Job, after God questions Job, then Job acknowledges that his wisdom is small compared to God's wisdom, and Job puts his hand over his mouth, no more questions! Job acknowledged he cannot answer God's questions to him.

> Behold, I am of small account; what shall I answer
> you? I lay my hand on my mouth.
>
> Job 40:4

Job then admits that he overdid it when he questioned God, and that he said things he did not understand.

> I know that you can do all things, and that no
> purpose of yours can be thwarted... Therefore I
> have uttered what I did not understand, things too
> wonderful for me, which I did not know.
>
> Job 42:2, 4

It is significant that shortly after Job's repentance we read that "the LORD restored the fortunes of Job, when he had prayed for his friends. And the LORD gave Job twice as much as he had before" (Job 42:10). When Job reached the absolute end of his own resources, then God restored his fortunes and gave him twice as much. When you and I reach the end of our resources and the end of our questioning God, then we are ready for the next significant step up the ladder of grace. Our humility must precede God's blessings.

How Is It That God is Good And Not Evil?

How is that we have a God who is good? How is it that the Bible can teach that God is a *good* God? How are we so blessed that God, who created all things, is morally and ethically good? What if God had turned out to be evil? Could it be that God is partially good and partially evil?

We simply do not have an answer to the question of how it is that God is a good God and not an evil God? All we can say is that the Bible teaches that God is good. The Bible does not give us an answer to the question of why or how God is good. Let us look at just a few of the Bible texts which teach that God is good:

> The Rock, his work is perfect, for all his ways are justice. A God of faithfulness and without iniquity, just and upright is he.
>
> Deuteronomy 32:4

> This God—his way is perfect; the word of the LORD proves true; he is a shield for all those who take refuge in him.
>
> 2 Samuel 22:31

> Great and amazing are your deeds, O Lord God the Almighty! Just and true are your ways, O King of the nations! Who will not fear, O Lord, and glorify your name? For you alone are holy.
>
> Revelation 15:3-4

I suggest we simply accept this teaching by faith, because the Bible says it is so, and that we give unlimited praise to God that he is good, was good, and will always be good!

So let us ask the question again, how is that God is a good God? The only answer found in the Bible is: Because God always chooses to do good. He could have chosen to be an evil God, but he chose to be good! Praise the Lord!

My Response To God's Claim Of Sovereignty

If we are not praising God more and more then this means that we do not believe in a sovereign God who always makes good and just decisions. How could I praise God more and more if I believe that a portion of the time he is making bad and unjust decisions?

May I suggest that you accept the Biblical description of a good sovereign God, and that you therefore praise him more and more. He wants what is best for me. I do not know which path in the future will be best for me, but he knows, so let him lead and direct. Do not be sidetracked by the many obstacles you can think of to having faith in this principle. The biggest advances we make in the Christian life come by faith. Not by sight, but by faith. Lord, I believe! One of the great benefits that comes from knowing the infinite God is that he will always do what is best for you. All of God's energy, all of God's resources, every aspect of his providence, is at work to bring about in your life what is best for you!

There is one Psalm above all the other Psalms that epitomizes the Lord's function in my life. It is the Twenty Third Psalm. It begins with the words: "The Lord is my Shepherd." The first responsibility of a Shepherd is to take good care of the sheep. The shepherd in Psalm 23 leads the sheep to green pastures and still waters. This was the best food available for the sheep. In between healthy meals, the shepherd guides them to rest in green pastures and leads his sheep in paths of righteousness. He protects them in the valley of the shadow of death, and from their enemies, staying by their side always. He surrounds them with goodness and mercy all the days of their lives.

Jesus knew that these were the responsibilities of the shepherd when he said, "I am the good shepherd" (John 10:10).

Jesus stood in the same relationship to his people as a shepherd does to his flock. He owns his people. Every one of his sheep belongs to him. He values every single one of his sheep. He protects them from the wolf. He guards them from a thousand dangers. He sees that they are a wandering flock, and so he is their strength. He calls them back when they wander. Without him who is our shepherd, we would wander further and farther away. We are in desperate need of his vigilance, and his watchful eye to call us back to himself. We are more dependent upon Christ than the sheep are upon the shepherd.

It is a challenge to believe that God is always working for good in my life. On May 14, 2020 I found myself studying Hebrews 13. When I reached Hebrews 13:20 the following thoughts came to me and I wrote them down in my diary:

> May 14, 2020. The words "working in you that which is well pleasing in his sight" shouted at me that even though I am feeling down, he is still working in me that which he desires to work in me. He is working in me that which is a part of my sanctification. He is doing what he wants to do in me. He is doing precisely what he wants to do in me and with me. He is sculpting me exactly as he desires to sculpt!! Yes, Lord Jesus, You are working in me exactly as You desire to work in me right now!! Yes, thank you!!! Lord, how could it be otherwise? You have promised to work in me "that which is well pleasing in your sight". You must be doing that at this very moment. Do I believe it? Right now? Yes, by the grace of God, by the might and power of the Holy Spirit, by the gracious will, and by the gracious choice of the Holy Spirit, you

are doing this right now!! This praising on my part
is a result of your working in me.

Will you join me now in affirming that all of God's dealings
with you are filled with his steadfast love. That every situation in
which God deals with you is marked by his steadfast love. That he
never deals with you in any way other than that of hesed. Yes, Lord
Jesus, thank you that every situation in which You deal with me is
marked by Your hesed, by your goodness, by Your steadfast love!!!
It is impossible for God to deal with me in any way other than
hesed, because this is his nature. But a crucial factor is: do I believe
it? Whether I believe it or not helps to determine the amount of joy
and peace that I experience. Yes Lord, I appropriate this magnificent
Biblical truth by believing it by faith.

When in the midst of trial and turbulence, give thanks with
enthusiastic exuberance! For he said, "I will never leave you, nor
forsake you (Hebrews 13:5)." In this promise, God gives to his people
everything. "I will never leave you." Then no attribute of God can
cease to be engaged for us. Is he strong? He will show himself strong
on behalf of them that trust him. Is he love? Then he will show love
toward us always. Whatever attributes may compose the character of
deity, every one of them to its fullest extent shall be engaged on our
side (For a fascinating commentary on this, see Jeremiah 32:41 "...
with all my heart and soul"). There is nothing you can want, there
is nothing you can ask for, there is nothing you will need in time
or in eternity, there is nothing now, nothing in heaven which is not
contained in this text: "I will never leave you, nor forsake you."

When we are in turbulent seas, let us not look to our feelings
and our human understanding as the grounds of our confidence, but
let us look to God's promises and providence. Let us look to God's
strength and to his steadfast love to guide us in our next step. There
is such a thing as "the devil's providences." When Jonah went down
to flee unto Tarshish, he found a ship going there; was not that a
remarkable providence? Perhaps Jonah said to himself, "I felt some

doubt about whether I was right in going there, but when I got down to the seashore, there was a ship, and there was just room for me to go as a passenger, and the fare was just the amount that I had, and so I felt that it must be of the Lord." Nonsense, Jonah. The Lord told you to go to Nineveh, not to Tarshish!" May God help you to carry out his will for you, and not to follow the false guideposts that are set in place by the devil in order to guide you away from God's will.

Will you affirm this with me now:

> I will make with them an everlasting covenant, that I will not turn away from doing good to them. And I will put the fear of me in their hearts, that they may not turn from me. I will rejoice in doing them good, and I will plant them in this land in faithfulness, with all my heart and all my soul.
>
> Jeremiah 32:40-41

For what reason did the Lord decide to be "my" shepherd? When David wrote the 23rd Psalm he knew that his Shepherd did all this for his name's sake (Psalm 23:3). The phrase "for his name's sake" is a theological phrase that is filled with deep meaning in the Old Testament. The Lord is our shepherd not because of anything that the sheep have done, or because the sheep have merited his shepherding them, but "for his name's sake!"

> He leads me beside still waters. He restores my soul. He leads me in paths of righteousness for his name's sake.
>
> Psalms 23:3

> But I acted for the sake of my name, that it should not be profaned in the sight of the nations among whom they lived, in whose sight I made myself

known to them in bringing them out of the land
of Egypt.

Ezekiel 20:9

But I acted for the sake of my name, that it should
not be profaned in the sight of the nations, in whose
sight I had brought them out.

Ezekiel 20:14

Yet he saved them for his name's sake, that he might
make known his mighty power.

Psalm 106:8

It is not for your sake, O house of Israel, that I am
about to act, but for the sake of my holy name,
which you have profaned among the nations to
which you came.

Ezekiel 36:22

Jesus decided to carry out all the functions of "The good
Shepherd" not because of anything the sheep have done or not done,
but for his own name's sake.

Yes, God wills what is best for me. What he desires from me is
that I believe this!

I can still remember the intense expectation I had when I was
waiting in line to see the movie "Star Wars" in 1977. At 8:53 a.m.,
my wife and our two children stood together in a line of a movie
theatre in Hollywood which went around the block. We were eagerly
looking forward to seeing the movie. We had heard so much, and
read so much about it. I do not remember any movie that had as
much pre-publicity as Star Wars. The excitement about actually
seeing this movie was building, rising like a crescendo, building to
a great climax. When I wake up in the morning, I often find myself

thinking about God's future for me during the rest of this day. What will it be? What will happen? What if I had the same positive, eager, anticipation that I had for seeing Star Wars? What if I believed that God was going to do something good, something wonderful? What if I could look at God's future for me with this same degree of eager, positive anticipation that I experienced as I waited to see Star Wars? Is this not what is promised to us when we read: "I will not turn away from doing good to them... I will bring upon them all the good that I promise them (Jeremiah 32:40, 32:42)."

I want to start believing he will do what is best for me, that I can rest in this with complete certainty ("God is not man, that he should lie...Has he said, and will he not do it? Numbers 23:19). It may not be what I would choose. It may not be what I think I want, but it will be what is best for me, because God always does what is best for me!!!

> No, in all these things we are more than conquerors through him who loved us.
>
> Romans 8:37

> But thanks be to God, who in Christ always leads us in triumphal procession, and through us spreads the fragrance of the knowledge of him everywhere
>
> 2 Corinthians 2:14

> But thanks be to God, who gives us the victory through our Lord Jesus Christ.
>
> 1 Corinthians 15:57

At times we are fearful of God's will. The biggest fear of many is: Lord, if I turn over my will to you, if I follow your will on this matter, perhaps I will miss out on something.. maybe I would be better off to follow my own will...maybe...

Let us praise him by being perfectly satisfied with everything he pours into our cup. Lord, I think you put too much salt in my cup. Did you leave out some sugar? Lord, everything You do is right whether I understand it or not, whether I agree with it or not. It is good and right, and it is the highest and the best. Oh Lord, if only I could believe with *all* my heart and soul that everything you do is good and right, why then of course I would praise you continually. Scripture tells me that's with all your heart and soul you endeavor to give me good things and do good to me. Is this not enough to persuade me that I can believe this to be true?

> I will make with them an everlasting covenant, that
> I will not turn away from doing good to them. And I
> will put the fear of me in their hearts, that they may
> not turn from me. I will rejoice in doing them good,
> and I will plant them in this land in faithfulness,
> *with all my heart and all my soul. (emphasis added)*
>
> Jeremiah 32:40-41

Scripture says that God gives us good things always, continually... *good things,* and that *he withholds no good thing from us.*

> For the LORD God is a sun and shield; the LORD
> bestows favor and honor. no good thing does he
> withhold from those who walk uprightly.
>
> Psalm 84:11

> For I know the plans I have for you, declares the
> LORD, plans for welfare and not for evil, to give you
> a future and a hope. For I know the plans I have for
> you, declares the LORD, plans for welfare and not
> for evil, to give you a future and a hope.
>
> Jeremiah 29:11

Well Walter, what would it take for you to believe that God will do in your life what the above Scriptures say God will do?

Because God does whatever he pleases, and because God is good, we could not be better off than we are now, all things considered, eternal things as well as present things. And if this truly be so, then with the Holy Spirit's help, I may begin to praise God enthusiastically at this very moment. This is my best response to God's sovereignty.

There once was a king of a mighty empire, and this powerful king picked *you* as his favorite subject. He was always doing you great favors, watching over your every need. He lavished great riches upon you every day. *Would you like to be a subject in such a kingdom?* This is what the Bible says it is like to be a follower of Jesus Christ, because Christ is sovereign, and he does whatever he pleases, and what pleases him is to do good always to his subjects. In this book, *More and More*, are principles which will show you how to grow more and more in your enjoyment of the riches of this kingdom.

He will always give good things. If you ask him for a fish, will he give you a serpent? If you ask him for bread will he give you poison. Go ahead and ask. He *desires* that you ask him. Is it not selfish to pray for bread? No, it is not selfish, for he desires that you ask for bread.

> For everyone who asks receives, and the one who seeks finds, and to the one who knocks it will be opened. What father among you, if his son asks for a fish, will instead of a fish give him a serpent; or if he asks for an egg, will give him a scorpion? If you then, who are evil, know how to give good gifts to your children, how much more will the heavenly Father give the Holy Spirit to those who ask him!"
>
> Luke 11:10-13

He will give the Holy Spirit, and good things to all who ask.

If you then, who are evil, know how to give good gifts to your children, how much more will your Father who is in heaven give good things to those who ask him!

Matthew 7:11

So then, Lord, do what you promised. You said. You promised that you will give good things to those who ask. You urged us to ask. So Lord, I believe that you will give me good things. Do Lord, as you have promised. Pour it on! Bring it on. I wait.

Where can I find such faith to believe that you will do as you have promised? Only in the Holy Spirit. Oh Holy Spirit, carry me into the stratosphere of this mighty faith. Carry me into the powerful faith you will fulfil all that you have promised. I call upon you now, O mighty Lord Jehovah!

A Symphonic Crescendo To A Great Biblical Teaching

Paul prayed the following for the new Christians at Ephesus:

...that you, being rooted and grounded in love, may have strength to comprehend with all the saints what is the breadth and length and height and depth, and to know the love of Christ that surpasses knowledge, that you may be filled with all the fullness of God.

Ephesians 3:17-19

The apostle said that the love of Christ surpasses knowledge. *This means that the love of Christ excels any cognitive description that can be given of it.*

The description of the "more and more" in this book attempts to describe the greatness of Christ, and our own experience of the

159

greatness of Christ. Paul told us that this description is far excelled by the reality of the thing itself!!! So our fullest description of the *"more and more"* in this book falls far short of the actuality of the love of Christ. And yet Paul says we are to *know* the love of Christ which passes knowledge. What a delightful paradox this is!

Paul tells us it is his desire, and the Lord's desire, that we attain to this fulness of experiencing God's love. Is God indeed able to bring this about? Yes, he is. This is precisely what Paul was praying for in Ephesians 3:17-19. Paul is praying that we might know the love of Christ which surpasses knowledge. Having said all this, our mind is staggered, and yet stretched even more, at the punctuation mark Paul places on this magnificent experience. For Paul says that once we accept and experience that Christ's love is so great that it surpasses knowledge, we have not yet attained the maximum love of Christ which it is possible for us to experience, for there yet remains *one more feat* that Christ is able to accomplish:

> Now to him who is able to do far more abundantly than all that we ask or think, according to the power at work within us.
>
> Ephesians 3:20

And that one more feat that God is able to accomplish is: "far more than all that we can ask or think!" So, ask and think! And praise him more and more for this one remaining feat that God is going to bring about, and which he is working on at this very moment.

But what if I do not make a full enough commitment to him? What if my faith is not quite strong enough, and not good enough, to fully believe in his ability to do what he said? The answer to this question is that *God* has made a new covenant with us. *This covenant is carried out successfully not by us, but by God.*

> Behold, the days are coming, declares the LORD,
> when I will make a new covenant with the house of
> Israel and the house of Judah, not like the covenant
> that I made with their fathers on the day when I
> took them by the hand to bring them out of the
> land of Egypt, my covenant that they broke, though
> I was their husband, declares the LORD. For this is
> the covenant that I will make with the house of
> Israel after those days, declares the LORD: I will
> put my law within them, and I will write it on their
> hearts. And I will be their God, and they shall be
> my people.
>
> Jeremiah 31:31-33

This new covenant does not depend on our obedience, like the first covenant that God made with our fathers when he led them out of Egypt. This new covenant centers on the bread and the cup of Jesus Christ, as stated by Jesus,

> And he took bread, and when he had given thanks,
> he broke it and gave it to them, saying, "This
> is my body, which is given for you. Do this in
> remembrance of me." And likewise the cup after
> they had eaten, saying, "This cup that is poured out
> for you is the new covenant in my blood."
>
> Luke 22:19-20

What if in my humanity I fail to keep my end of the covenant? The new covenant has no dependency upon *my* obedience to God's commandments. Christ is my representative. Christ is my righteousness, and my hope, and my salvation. Christ has fulfilled the human side of the covenant by perfectly representing me! It is not possible for Christ to fail in what he has promised. Has he not said, and will he not do it? So, in Christ, God will perfectly fulfill his covenant with me. With this commitment from God, I can praise him more and more that his covenant will be fulfilled in me, abundantly, and far beyond my greatest hope!

Fulfilling his covenant means that this covenant on his part is everlasting. God will never break his covenant with me. He will always do good to me, he will never cease doing good to me.

Does this mean that his covenant with me is independent of what I do, and that I can do whatever I desire? No, because the Lord said, "For this is the covenant that I will make with the house of Israel after those days, declares the LORD: I will put my law within them, and I will write it on their hearts. And I will be their God, and they shall be my people (Jeremiah 31:31-33)." He puts his laws within our hearts *so that we will desire to do his will.*

> I will make with them an everlasting covenant, that I will not turn away from doing good to them. And I will put the fear of me in their hearts, that they may not turn from me. I will rejoice in doing them good, and I will plant them in this land in faithfulness, with all my heart and all my soul.
>
> Jeremiah 32:40-41

Yes, I can therefore have absolute assurance that God will always behave toward me in the most loving manner possible.

Let us look again at the words "more and more" in Psalms 71:14. As you read Psalm 71, it is clear that the writer of this psalm speaks of a life that has faced many trials, and that the writer is approaching the evening of life.

> [9] Do not cast me off in the time of old age; forsake me not when my strength is spent...
>
> [14] But I will hope continually and will praise you yet more and more...

¹⁷ O God, from my youth you have taught me, and I still proclaim your wondrous deeds...

¹⁸ So even to old age and gray hairs, O God, do not forsake me, until I proclaim your might to another generation, your power to all those to come....

²⁰ You who have made me see many troubles and calamities will revive me again; from the depths of the earth you will bring me up again.

Portions of Psalm 71:9-20

The writer of Psalm 71 is in the time of "old age."(vs 9). From my youth you have taught me. The writer remembers past days of youth (vs. 17), and mentions "old age" again in vs. 18, and says "many troubles and calamities" (vs 20). This is the context of the statement "I will praise you more and more."

It is extremely significant that in this context the writer is able to say "I will praise you more and more." What this says to us is that even if I am advanced in age, and have been through many trials, I can make the audacious statement that I will praise God "more and more." This means I will praise God more than I ever have before. We go hurtling into two infinities here. The first infinity is in the phrase "I will praise you yet more and more," because the amount of praise I can give God is not at a fixed level, nor does it *decrease* with our advancing age, but it continues to increase, more and more, more today than yesterday, and more tomorrow than today. So the amount of praise that I am going to give God is ever increasing. Over time, "ever increasing" is a good definition of infinity.

The second infinity is within God himself. It is his greatness, it is the praise that is due him on our behalf. And it is the power of the Holy Spirit that is able to bathe us in the unsearchable riches of Jesus Christ. And these two infinities meet in the full glory of the face of God in Jesus Christ (2 Corinthians 4:6), and this explosion of glory is something that you and I participate in now, by praising him. More and more.

Do you want this kind of life? Where you can praise him more and more? Tell him. This is a prayer which God delights to answer! Tell him now.

> Lord, I want to praise you more and more. Make whatever changes you need to make in me so that I will praise you more and more. I ask this in the name of Jesus Christ. Amen.

Hold on to your seat, for you are about to begin a new ride, a new journey in your life...a journey where you will begin to praise him more and more, and more.

And better thence again, and better still, in infinite progression...

More and More

I will hope continually, and will praise you yet more and more.

Psalm 71:14

APPENDIX –
THE BOOK COVER

Admittedly it is unusual for an artistic rendition in astronomy to grace the cover of a book on spiritual formation. For this reason I have included a brief comment in this appendix. The artist is my grandson, Lucas Lovejoy, who has just graduated from New York University. The cover artwork is a rendition of "The Big Bang," in conjunction with the Cross of Jesus Christ.

The Big Bang is a theory about the origin of the universe that says there was a cosmic explosion at an instant of time roughly 14 billion years ago. All the matter in the universe at that time fit into an object smaller than an atom. Since that time our universe has been expanding to its present condition. Talking about the Big Bang theory, Alan Guth of MIT says: "...this theory is now generally accepted by almost all scientists actively working in cosmology."[25]

The Cross of Christ plays a part in the artistic depiction of the Big Bang, since the Gospel of John says that all things were made by and through Jesus Christ, and the subject of this book is how we can grow in our relationship with Jesus Christ.

> In the beginning was the Word, and the Word was with God, and the Word was God. He was in the beginning with God. All things were made through

---

[25] Op.cit., p.34

him, and without him was not any thing made that
was made.

John 1:1-2

"The Word" in John 1:1-2 clearly is a reference to Jesus Christ,
for we read in John 1:14 "and the Word became flesh."

For this reason, the big bang and the Cross are shown together
on the cover of this book. An aspect of each is captured by the title
of the book: "more and more." As the overall size of the universe
continues to expand (more and more; in fact, at an accelerating
rate, to the surprise of physicists), so the quality and intensity of our
relationship with Christ can grow "more and more," hence a reason
for depicting the Big Bang and the Cross of Christ together, as one...
both growing in their influence...more and more.

Printed in the United States
by Baker & Taylor Publisher Services